Norman Foster

Norman Foster
A Global Architecture

Martin Pawley

 Thames & Hudson

First published in the United Kingdom in 1999 by
Thames & Hudson Ltd, 181A High Holborn,
London WC1V 7QX

Reprinted 2001

British Library Cataloguing-in-Publication Data
A catalogue record for this book is available
from the British Library

ISBN 0-500-28123-8

Printed and bound in Italy

Contents

Introduction   6

Projects   20   Reliance Controls Electronics Factory, Swindon, England

28   Computer Technology and Fred Olsen Buildings, Hemel Hempstead and London, England

40   IBM Pilot Head Office, Cosham, England, and IBM Technical Park, Greenford, England

50   Willis Faber and Dumas Headquarters, Ipswich, England

58   Sainsbury Centre for Visual Arts and Crescent Wing, University of East Anglia, Norwich, England

68   Renault Distribution Centre, Swindon, England

74   Hongkong and Shanghai Bank Headquarters, Hong Kong, China, and Century Tower, Tokyo, Japan

84   Nomos Furniture System

88   Projects with Richard Buckminster Fuller

92   Carré d'Art, Nîmes, France, and Cranfield University Library, Bedfordshire, England

102   BBC Radio Centre, London, England

108   ITN Headquarters, London, England

114   Foster and Partners Studios, Battersea, London, England

120   Passenger Terminal and Satellites, Third London Airport, Stansted, England

130   Hong Kong International Airport Passenger Terminal, Hong Kong, China

142   Duisburg Energy-Efficient Buildings, Duisburg, Germany: Business Promotion Center, Telematic Center, Microelectronic Center

156   Telecommunications Facilities, Barcelona and Santiago de Compostela, Spain

164   Millennium Tower Projects, Tokyo, Japan, and London, England

170   Commerzbank Headquarters, Frankfurt, Germany

178   Sackler Galleries, Royal Academy of Arts, London, England, and American Air Museum, Imperial War Museum, Duxford, England

190   Faculty of Law, University of Cambridge, Cambridge, England

196   Scottish Exhibition and Conference Centre, Glasgow, Scotland

204   Congress Center, Valencia, Spain

210   Lycée Albert Camus, Fréjus, France

216   National Botanic Garden of Wales, Llanarthne, Wales

220   Great Court, British Museum, London, England

228   New German Parliament, Reichstag, Berlin, Germany

Foster and Partners
Principal Projects   236
Photography Credits   240

Introduction

Glasgow's docklands in wintertime is not everybody's cup of tea. Freezing rain blows across deserted quays and empty basins. Tattered strips of fabric flutter from a chainlink fence, the remnants of an advertising banner from the previous summer. At such times, in such places, the idea of urban renewal seems a contradiction in terms, and the task of architecture in promoting it quite impossible. Here there seems nothing to renew, nothing except a landscape of desolation symbolized by an eternally inert dockside crane.

But a determined search for any cause for optimism is generously rewarded. One object in particular is a harbinger of things to come: a glistening silver shape partly hidden by newly planted trees (wisely tethered down against the wind), which consists of superimposed curved metal arches that resemble a giant metal armadillo. This is the 3,000-seat Industrial Theatre and Exhibition Hall of the Scottish Exhibition and Conference Centre, designed by Sir Norman Foster.

On this particular winter's day the architect himself is inside the building, explaining the logic behind its unusual shape to a group of journalists. As usual he speaks unhurriedly and with precision. Summing up the rationale of what is now universally called 'the Armadillo' he says: "This is an industrial theater and so it would be appropriate if it were an industrial building, but it is not. It is almost an industrial building. It is a mixture of cultural form and industrial technology that allows a skin of zero-maintenance aluminum to be shrink-wrapped around the shape of an auditorium at half the cost of a conventional building envelope." His audience is silent.

"Isn't there any downside to using industrial cladding materials like this, instead of stone or concrete?" someone asks.

"Only one," Sir Norman smiles. "Some people say the building looks like the Sydney Opera House."

Whether it looks like the Sydney Opera House or not, the Industrial Theatre in Glasgow shares none of its antipodean counterpart's troubled history. This building achieves its value by ingenuity of design rather than by lavish expenditure. Structurally it consists of a precast and bonded concrete block auditorium that anchors a series of curved tubular steel trusses, over which are "flopped" great parallelograms of profiled aluminum sheet. During construction this industrial cladding material arrived on site in giant rolls that, when in place, fell naturally into a counterprofile curvature identical to that of a cylinder 38 meters in diameter. The ingenuity and precision of this arrangement, which required no complicated rebending of a standard-profile industrial material, made genuine savings possible without losing the architectural invention typical—and now even expected—of Foster's office.

The Armadillo is "almost" an industrial building in several ways, not least in the economy with which it achieves its grand effects. As the architect points out, the only expensive assembly in the whole design is the tall glass screen wall that rises above the main entrance doors. Everything else, from the painted finish of the concrete auditorium to the extensive interior use of medium-density fiberboard, is plain and hard—so much plainer and harder than an industrial building would dare to be that it almost enters the category of military architecture. But again only "almost," for this is military architecture modulated by an elegance of form and precision of assembly that produced not only aesthetic satisfaction, but a construction cost of less than $42 million for 13,000 square meters of highly serviced conference and exhibition space. The facility was completed ahead of schedule and was booked for conferences and conventions five years in advance on the day it opened. Given this list of plusses, can there be any argument against the skillful use of industrial materials to clad important public buildings? The question cannot be answered, for everything resides in the qualification "almost," and that is the contribution of genius.

The Glasgow "Armadillo," which opened for business in spring 1998, is one of the smaller buildings designed by Foster and Partners in recent years. At the opposite end of the scale are such contemporaneous giants as the $800 million, 10,000-square-meter Commerzbank headquarters in Frankfurt—a financial services skyscraper completed in 1997 that, at nearly 260 meters, is the tallest building in Europe—and the $20 billion passenger terminal at Hong Kong International Airport, with its three miles of external glazing, a concourse three-fourths of a mile long, and forty-five acres of barrel-vaulted, self-supporting space-frame roof. Completing this triad of recent large projects is a commission just as grand but very different in appearance and history: the $450 million reconstruction of the Reichstag, the most prestigious public commission the German government has ever awarded a non-German architect.

The first of these great structures, the Frankfurt Commerzbank, exploits the capabilities of geometry in a manner similar to that devised for the Glasgow Exhibition and Conference Centre. Besides being one of the most advanced high-rise buildings in the world, with its sky gardens operating with an advanced natural-ventilation system, the structure of this building is based on a triangular plan, with all vertical structural elements, elevators, staircases, and service corridors confined to the corners of the triangle, so that there is no central structural core but instead a full-height atrium that acts as a ventilation funnel. The building also features four-story gardens that run from corner to corner spiralling around the three sides of the triangle to give attractive views on each floor.

The terminal at Hong Kong International Airport also incorporates an ingenious geometry, in the design of its enormous oversailing steel diagonal grid roof, which is supported by widely spaced reinforced-concrete columns. The focus of the greatest concentration of design expertise in the building, the undulating roof was assembled from site-welded steel lattice shells, each nearly 1,300 square meters in area. In addition to devising an elegant structure, Foster and Partners and their structural engineers, Ove Arup & Partners, reduced the number of components to an almost unbelievably small kit of standard parts that was capable of meeting every possible edge, condition, or junction. The diagonal grid roof structure itself, for example, was assembled from thousands of identical steel beams that were welded together at precise angles on site on special jigs to produce the barrel-vaulted sections, which weigh more than 130 tons each. These were then lifted by computer-controlled cranes and placed in their final positions on top of the supporting columns.

Foster modestly explained this achievement: "It is a large but extremely economical roof. All the structural members are standard steel sections, delivered cut to the same length. The longitudinal and lateral changes of slope in the roof don't need special components because the sliding bolted joints over the supporting columns were specially designed to absorb very large tolerances." In other words, the roof is a self-regulating mechanism.

The third great commission carried out by Foster and Partners in recent years, the reconstruction of the former Reichstag in Berlin, represented challenges historical as well as structural. Just over one hundred years old, the Reichstag was designed in the classical style by a Frankfurt architect named Paul Wallot. For various reasons, Wallot's building did not become the nation's parliament until 1920, and then served as the chamber of the democratically elected German government for only thirteen years, until the suspension of parliament. In 1933 it was rendered unusable by a fire that helped the Nazis' rise to power, and ten years later it was almost totally destroyed by bombing during World War II.

Given this troubled history, the German government's decision to rebuild the Reichstag, made in the aftermath of reunification, presented numerous problems.

The ensuing architectural competition, open to all German architects as well as to invited foreigners, proved unpopular; only eighty firms submitted designs. Foster was apprehensive when he found out he'd been included on the small list of non-German architects invited to compete. "I did not see how Germany could go outside its borders to get this symbolic job done," he confessed later. But he was wrong. The honor fell to him and he grasped the symbolism of the building with both hands. His competition design placed a vast glass canopy over the battered walls of the Reichstag, as though to insulate it from a dubious past. No historically aware German could fail to understand this gesture. It contrived somehow to preserve an inauspicious national emblem while at the same time giving it a new and more positive meaning.

Considerable politicking, alterations, and economizing were required before the German parliament was prepared to commission Foster and Partners to carry out this delicate transformation. The glass canopy was abandoned, though the concepts of transparency and daylighting were retained. A more modest scheme, to take place within the walls of the old building, was devised. The interior was drastically 'clarified', a process that involved removing 12,000 tons of rubble, restoring the original number of floors, reopening all four original entrances, and rebuilding two inner courtyards. The result has been a radical transformation of the gloomy, war-scarred building.

Naturally assisted ventilation and an extensive use of daylighting characterize the new Reichstag, features that depend heavily on the use of quantities of high-performance glass. The dominant glass structure is a cupola over parliament's debating chamber, taking the place of the original copper and glass dome. This cupola encloses a 23-meter-tall inverted cone fitted with 360 mirrors that direct daylight down into the debating chamber and reflect views of the sky.

Riverside Three

The studios of Foster and Partners, though involved in projects worldwide, are firmly headquartered in London, in a combined office and apartment building called Riverside Three, designed by Foster. Conceived in the mid-1980s, Riverside Three is of uncompromisingly modern appearance. Prominently located on the south bank of the Thames in Battersea, overlooking the river between the Albert and Battersea Bridges, the near-rectangular eight-story concrete frame structure presents a pale-white and greenish glass face to the northern horizon. Except when approached by water, reaching Riverside Three requires a journey from the southern abutment of Battersea Bridge down a neglected street lined with desolate 'development opportunities.' The building's entrance opens onto an arrow-straight, cinematically long series of stairs that terminates at the building's second level, which gives access to a vast, double-height studio space flanked on one side by a long mezzanine balcony. Above this bustling studio are five floors of apartments unconnected with the offices, and above them, occupying almost all of the roof, is a penthouse. This dwelling, with its spectacular panorama of the London skyline, is the home of Sir Norman Foster and his family.

Foster and Partners' studio at Riverside Three is confined to the first, second, and mezzanine levels of the main building, though there is also a smaller two-story building to the rear. The first and second levels in the main building are rectangles encompassing over 14,000 square meters; both are given over entirely to the multifarious business of architecture: computer-aided design, drafting, model making, and discussion. The lower of the two levels has daylighting from the north side only, a much lower ceiling, and other adaptations for intensive computer use.

The contrast with the level above is profound—the studio is a brightly daylit, double-height space best appreciated from its mezzanine balcony, which provides a view that can hardly be matched by any other architects' office in the world. Because the tall glass walls at each end of the rectangular space—roughly east- and west-facing—are shaded by stretched fabric blinds, and because the view to the rear is blocked by staircases, meeting rooms, and support areas, all attention is directed to the front, which presents an unobstructed panorama of the River Thames and the Chelsea embankment on the northern bank beyond. Remarkable though this view is, it can hardly compare with the scene below. On the studio floor are thirteen immense island drawing tables, each covered with computer monitors, files, books, and papers interspersed with fragments of models and examples of building components. Lining these great tables, sitting and standing

The studio floor at Foster and Partners is filled with thirteen immense drawing tables, each covered with monitors, files, books, and papers.

back to back, are the architects and assistants at work. From the mezzanine it is impossible to guess the status of any one of them, the crowd comprising a mixture of directors, associates, employees, clients, and visitors. At Foster and Partners, there are no private offices, nor is a uniform dress code enforced or implied. A kind of democracy reigns. Some people wear suits and ties, some are in shirtsleeves, some in jeans and sweaters, but all work alongside one another in an environment that is as reminiscent of a currency dealing room as it is of most people's idea of an architects' office. The only real difference is that the ambient noise level is reduced to the dull murmur of an airport lounge by the height and volume of the huge space.

Even if certain of his presence, a visitor on the balcony would have great difficulty in locating Sir Norman Foster on this immense designing floor. Like all the directors and associates of the firm he has no private office, only a location. In his case this a white circular table in the northeastern corner of the room, as far from the entrance as it is possible to get. Indeed, his table can be reached only by threading past the ends of the long cantilevered drawing tables that stand like piers waiting for great ships to dock. Sir Norman is often to be seen at this table, deep in conversation, plying one of the black, hardbound sketchbooks and soft pencils that he uses as a visual aid while he talks. These sketchbooks are his constant companions. In his library there are rows of them on metal shelves, filed in chronological order, the oldest dating back to the dawn of his architectural career, when his studio was the front room of a flat in London's Belsize Park.

Nearly forty years later, Foster's studio at Riverside Three has become the focal point of an organization responsible for hundreds of millions of dollars worth of design work worldwide. From this commanding yet subtly democratic position at a round table in the corner of his great studio—where merely by standing up he can see some 150 of his people at work, in front of monitors, on the telephone, in impromptu conference, studying models, or simply drawing—he and his fellow directors run a global enterprise. As of September 1998, Foster and Partners employed 491 persons, 400 of them located in Riverside Three, the others dotted across the world: Hong Kong, Berlin, Singapore, Dusseldorf, Tokyo, Glasgow, and elsewhere. In the thirty-two years since the formation of Foster Associates, his firm has undertaken more than 1,000 projects, won some 130 design awards, and projected the name of its founder into the select company of the greatest architects of the twentieth century.

Sir Norman Foster

Norman Foster was born into a working-class family in the industrial city of Manchester in 1935. Academically undistinguished, he left school at sixteen and found a job as a clerical assistant in the city treasurer's office, followed by two years of military service in the Royal Air Force. It was not until he was in his twenties that he enrolled, without financial assistance, at Manchester University to study architecture. His design abilities were soon recognized.

He recalled those early years when accepting an honorary doctorate from his old university in 1993. "For a long time," he said, "I believed I came from a poor background because I had to work to pay my way through university at the same time as studying. But I was wrong. All the things I thought were barriers turned out be incentives. The best favor Manchester ever did for me was to refuse me a grant."

The year Foster graduated from Manchester he won a Henry Fellowship to study at Yale, where he met and befriended another English student, Richard Rogers, also destined to achieve great success. At Yale as at Manchester, his formidable qualities as a designer were quickly recognized, and he earned his masters degree without difficulty. Influenced by the great American design guru Richard Buckminster Fuller (with whom he was later to collaborate on several projects), as well as such distinguished tutors as Paul Rudolph, Serge Chermayeff, and the critic Vincent Scully, Foster learned a great deal during his time in America. When he returned to England in 1963 he was a man transformed. He had become a self-motivated perfectionist with a new energy and ambition. His own explanation for this change came out in another acceptance speech. "In England I was the odd one out," he told his audience in Washington, D.C., when he received the American Institute of Architects Gold Medal in 1994. "Working-class background, early-school-leaver, a place in the university but no grant. I was an outsider. But when I came here I felt that I had come home. There was a pride in working and serving. I felt liberated. It is no exaggeration to say that I discovered myself through America."

On their return to England, he and Richard Rogers set up practice together as Team 4. In love with the lightness and simplicity of American welded steel construction, they designed (with the engineer Anthony Hunt) the now demolished Reliance Controls building in Swindon, a perfect American steel-box factory building. But their partnership was not to last: they separated in 1967. Foster founded Foster Associates and began to make a name for himself as an industrial architect, working with lightweight materials and novel techniques to create facilities for the new industries that were beginning

An impromptu conference. Like all his directors and associates Foster has no private office, only a location.

to burgeon all over England. In 1969 he gave a magazine interview that revealed the astonishing scale of his ambitions and the extent of his boundless confidence in the structural potential of modern architecture, as well as the exuberant mood of the time. "Vast areas will soon be enclosed with lightweight space-frame structures or inflatable plastic membranes," he predicted. "Full climatic control is feasible; the polar regions can be tropicalized and desert areas cooled."

While some ambitious schemes of this sort did linger and recur on the firm's drawing boards, most did not. In the 1970s Foster was rapidly graduating from metal sheds on industrial estates to office buildings of an entirely new type for major corporations such as IBM and the insurance brokers Willis Faber and Dumas. Then, with the patronage of the powerful Sainsbury family, Foster produced his first major cultural building, the Sainsbury Centre for Visual Arts at the University of East Anglia. This elegant structure looked so perfect in its verdant setting—"like a cigarette lighter on a billiard table," as the narrator of a BBC documentary put it—that the world beyond England began to take notice. By the end of the decade Foster Associates had won international competitions to design new headquarters for the Hongkong and Shanghai Bank in Hong Kong and for BBC Radio in central London; was designing a major parts distribution center for Renault; was about to start work on the design of a media center and library in Nîmes, France; and had begun the ten-year project that was to culminate in a spectacular passenger terminal at London's Stansted Airport.

In the mythology of Foster and Partners, the crucial period in the development of the practice is the early 1980s. The Renault project was winding down but the Hongkong and Shanghai Bank and BBC Radio buildings both demanded considerable increases in staff as well as a newer and larger London office. In what looked like a severe blow at the time, the BBC project was abruptly canceled, the result of a sudden economic slump and the death of the project's chief advocate. But that disappointment seems now to have had a silver lining. Opposition to modern projects was running high in England, and the BBC project promised a vicious battle between the architect and preservation interests, a battle the architect could well have lost.

For any student of Foster's career, there is no question that the Hongkong and Shanghai Bank marked the turning point in his fortunes. It is still famous as one of the most expensive buildings of modern times with a popularly quoted budget of $600 million for its forty-one stories and 100,000 square meters of floor space. The commission to design the bank was won at a time when (it is now remembered with amazement) the firm had never built a building more than three stories high. Undeterred by this lack of experience, in 1979 the firm set up an office in Hong Kong, staffed at first with twelve people sent out from London under director Spencer de Grey. Twelve proved to be an underestimate of the staff needed; the project continued to mushroom until the office had 150 people.

By the time the building was completed in 1986, the Foster office had taught itself all it needed to know about high-rise construction. Their Hongkong and Shanghai Bank emerged as a steel-framed tower 180 meters high. Of extremely elaborate and very precise design, it was divided structurally into three transverse bays and five vertical zones. The floors within each vertical zone were suspended from bridge-like structures shaped like cranes that stretched between the steel masts at the bridges' corners. The elegance of this solution to obtaining a core-free interior rests in the balance of structural and nonstructural elements on each facade. For despite the perversity of its long-span structural system, the clarity of the relationship between the exoskeletal structural members and the "boxes" within enabled the building to explain its own structure in a far more satisfying manner than the conventional high rises that surround it.

The saga of the Hongkong and Shanghai Bank involved virtually every Foster employee at some point between 1979 and 1986. The firm's senior partners vividly remember that period today; Spencer de Grey, David Nelson, Graham Phillips, and Ken Shuttleworth all worked on the project. The difficulties involved in designing, specifying, and building such a complicated structure on the other side of the world not only taught the designers important lessons, it also gave the firm a head start in the market for modern, intelligent buildings in the Far East, which was just beginning to emerge. More important still was the way in which the bank produced a steady stream of income during the savage European recession of the early 1980s, when construction work in Britain practically ceased. By 1986, when the Hongkong and Shanghai Bank opened, Norman Foster was already designing Century Tower, an innovative commercial high rise in Tokyo. More Far East commissions eventually led to Hong Kong International Airport at Chek Lap Kok and the formation of a project office called Foster Asia in Hong Kong in 1993.

By the end of the 1980s, Norman Foster had become an international celebrity and a symbol of contemporary architecture. Showered with commissions and competition wins, he undertook projects and opened project offices in Duisburg, Berlin, Frankfurt, Paris, Hong Kong, Singapore, and Tokyo, in each place demonstrating his mastery of every branch of architecture—except one, historical preservation. Unlike most English architects, Norman Foster had been preoccupied with overseas work at the height of Prince Charles's interventions into British architecture in the mid-1980s. But Foster's seeming lack of concern for preservation turned out to be a false impression. In a small way, his chance to show what he could do in this area had already come, and he had already seized it.

When they were opened by Her Majesty the Queen in June 1991, the new Sackler Galleries Foster had designed at the Royal Academy of Arts—a prestigious institution occupying the seventeenth-century Burlington House in London's Piccadilly—were not universally admired. The critics from the *Spectator* and the *Catholic Herald* objected, the former comparing his creation of a daylit sculpture gallery to "Fellini's bathroom," and the latter likening the picture galleries to "operating theaters cum squash courts." Since then, however, these voices have been overwhelmed by praise. For although Norman Foster was knighted in 1990 for his services to architecture following the triumphant completion of the huge passenger terminal at Stansted Airport, the project that finally charmed the English establishment into accepting his genius was this much more modest work.

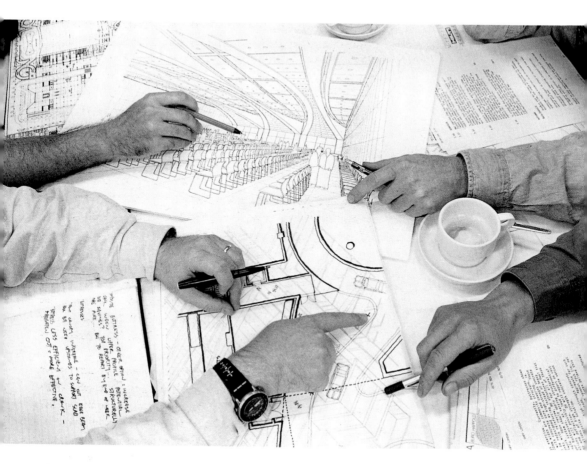

In the studio, directors, architects, and associates all work together.

To date the galleries have received fourteen national and international awards. And Foster and Partners' critical success has been rewarded financially, too. The $160 million commission for alterations to the British Museum, the new wing of the Joslyn Arts Museum in Omaha, Nebraska, and the $450 million commission to remodel the Reichstag all came, in part at least, as a result of the modest $8 million reorganization of the galleries at the Royal Academy.

The Sackler Galleries project had begun unpromisingly in 1985 as an invitation to refurbish three decrepit Victorian galleries in Burlington House. Foster saw from the outset that there would be little benefit in improving the old galleries without improving the means of access to them, which was hopelessly inadequate. He looked for a better line of approach, which he found in the gap between the original Burlington House and the gallery extension added by Sidney Smirke in 1867. Opening up that gap exposed the garden facade of Burlington House, not seen for more than a century, as well as the south wall of Smirke's extension. Foster restored both these facades to their original state and inserted between them a freestanding structure that contained a new staircase and elevator. He also created a new glass-enclosed sculpture gallery at the top of that gap. The result was a perfect combination of old and new, a solution with a directness and honesty evident to every visitor.

In December 1992, a year after the opening of the Sackler Galleries, Foster was invited to speak at a seminar on 'Conservation in Architecture' at the Royal Institute of British Architects. To those who had watched the polarity between the modernists and the traditionalists intensify for years, the only thing more amazing than this Christmas truce was the triumphant architect's acceptance of it. Twenty-three years after he had written about a new high-tech architecture that could enclose cities, warm ice caps, and cool deserts, Norman Foster held this audience spellbound with tales of the rediscovery of a long-hidden garden facade, the reinsertion of a once deleted window, and the poignancy of a nineteenth-century elevation, lovingly detailed even though no one would ever see it. This was a new Norman Foster, still an architect with attitude, but an architect with respect, too, a respect for the past that, like his vision of the future, has opened doors all over the world.

Today, at the age of sixty-three, with more than thirty years of practice in his own name, Norman Foster still needs new worlds to conquer. His tiny, back-room studio has grown into an enormous international concern. At the time of this writing, Foster and Partners had projects in Britain, France, Germany, Saudi Arabia, China, Japan, and the United States, among many other countries. Currently, his attention is drawn to the progress of the glass roof he has designed to enclose the Great Court of the British Museum. Of these triumphs and challenges, and those that have come before, perhaps the last is the sweetest and the best, not only because of its prestige, but also because it marks the surrender of the English establishment to his vision. Without compromising his own genius, Norman Foster has bypassed the political booby traps, the notoriously cautious, middle-of-the-road aesthetics, and the old school ties of English privilege to glide adroitly to the front rank.

Reliance Controls Electronics Factory
Swindon, England, 1966

The Reliance Controls factory was a joint creation of four architects under the age of thirty—Norman Foster, Richard Rogers, and Wendy and Georgie Cheesman—then practicing under the name Team 4, along with the structural engineer Anthony Hunt. Its completion coincided with the break-up of Team 4 and the formation of Foster Associates in 1967. The factory survived for only twenty-five years; it was demolished in 1991 despite a televised appeal to preservation authorities that it should be protected because of the originality and historical importance of its design.

The factory was built on an industrial estate on the outskirts of Swindon, a provincial town some eighty miles west of London. The building presented a radical alternative to the front-management-office/back-production-shed structure that was the norm for English light industrial architecture at the time. There was a single entrance for management and employees alike, and a single restaurant.

In addition to its sociological and organizational innovations, Reliance Controls represented a unique fusion of American and

External cross bracing, below, and
Miesian painted steelwork, opposite page.

Following pages: the combined elements
with paved entrance area.

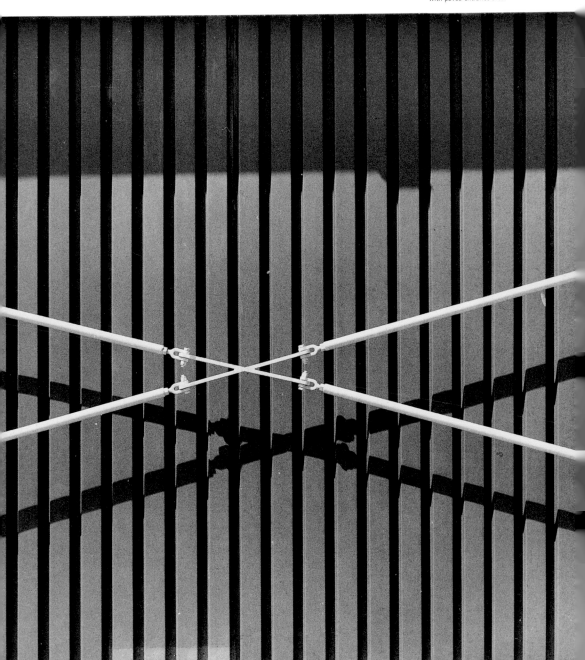

European thinking about factory design. Windowless on three sides, the building's hot-rolled welded steel structural frame, based on a long-span, 40-square-foot grid, was expressed externally to dramatic effect. With all main structural members painted white, including diagonal rod bracing that stood out against the dark gray, plastic-coated steel cladding behind it, the design attempted to reconcile the precise domestic aesthetic of Mies van der Rohe's Farnsworth House with the Brutalism of Alison and Peter Smithson's Hunstanton School. When the building received the first *Financial Times* Architecture at Work award in 1967, the jurors wrote that the architects had "discovered a lost vernacular"; at about the same time, the Italian magazine *Casabella* called the building an example of "assembly without composition."

Originally intended as the first and second phases of a much larger structure, the 3,200-square-meter rectangular metal box offered a single, subdividable, multifunctional, production space. From the outset, the designers proposed that additional bays could be added to the building without interrupting production;

Perspective sections, below and opposite, showing structural elements.

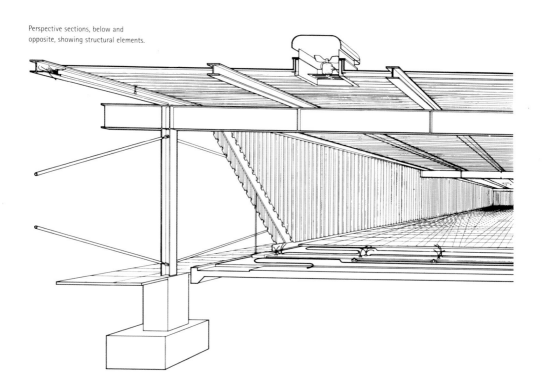

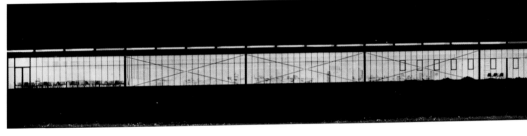

Exterior view of glazed facade at night.

Elevation to main road.

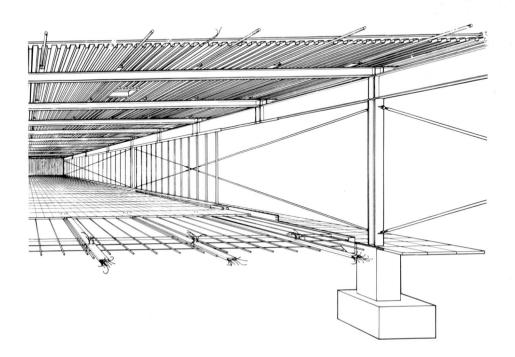

Interior of production area showing
removable glass partitioning.

on one occasion early in the building's life another 800 square meters of floor space were added. Within the original rectangle, only the kitchens, toilets, and plant room were in fixed locations. The distribution of other services, including heating and compressed air, was by means of a single large floor duct and multiple ceiling ducts.

Although a shared commission, Reliance Controls incorporated or hinted at many of the innovations Norman Foster was to bring to industrial and commercial architecture over the following three decades: a rational deep-plan design for minimal superstructure surface area; large module, clear-span steel construction with light metal cladding; the minimization of wet trades; the extensive use of metal components for quick construction; a multifunctional internal space that could be reconfigured rapidly; a rational distribution of services from above and below; and, last but not least, workplace democracy achieved through design.

Principal consultants: Anthony Hunt, structural engineers; G.N. Haden & Sons Ltd., service engineers; Hanscomb Partnership, cost consultants

Interior perspective sketch by Norman Foster.

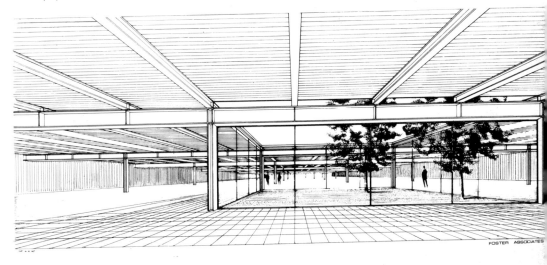

Computer Technology
and Fred Olsen Buildings
Hemel Hempstead and London, England, 1968-71

The arrival of 'clean' industries at the end of the 1960s created a new kind of client for factory buildings and thus an opportunity for a new architecture. After the completion of Reliance Controls and the breakup of Team 4, the newly formed Foster Associates was commissioned by one such clean-industry client, a company called Computer Technology, to design a four-phase program on a site in Hemel Hempstead, a satellite town north of London.

The first two phases involved altering and refurbishing a former canning factory for the production of printed circuit boards. False ceilings were designed to create a 'service zone' for lighting and electrical distribution from above and, as a modest but extremely effective innovation, production areas were carpeted to reduce noise.

The third phase involved creating temporary offices. Foster proposed a nylon and PVC-fabric inflatable structure that would accommodate seventy employees for one year. Designed, manufactured, and installed in twelve weeks, the translucent structure was inflated in a parking lot. Inside, the inflatable building was carpeted and equipped with conventional office furniture as well as a number of inclined lighting stanchions angled so as to bounce light off the envelope as well as to support it in the event of damage or collapse. Electricity was supplied to all workstations from a main circuit that encircled the perimeter atop a poured-concrete beam. During the twelve months this building was in use, it served as a testing ground for various means of heating and cooling, including twin oil-fired air heaters, portable air-conditioning units, and evaporative water sprays for the exterior. At about $1.20 per square foot, this was undoubtedly the cheapest building Foster ever designed.

The final phase of the Computer Technology project was the

Interior of the inflatable.

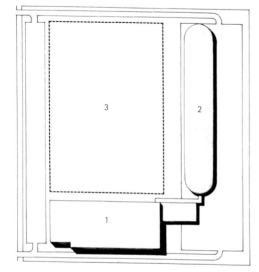

Site plan showing:
1 Converted canning factory
2 Air supported temporary offices
3 New building

Exterior of new building.

Part of the original canning factory
before, left, and after, right.

Computer Technology and Fred Olsen Buildings

Montage of structural, cladding, and site elements.

Interior of the new building, opposite page, showing glazing and service zone.

design of a permanent research and development building. Drawing on experience gained at Reliance Controls, Foster designed a rectangular, 13,000-square-meter, deep-plan building. It was a steel-framed, single-story structure with vertical stanchions supporting long-span castellated beams on a 13-by-13-meter grid. Air-conditioning units were roof-mounted directly above the main structural beams to minimize vibration.

The architects assumed that there would never be a need for full-height partitions inside the building, and so did not design a false ceiling. All servicing took place within the roof zone, with color-coded service connections threading through the castellated beams as necessary. Below this 'servicing umbrella', the continuous perimeter glass cladding rose from floor level to above head height. Above the glass line, aluminum-faced polyurethane panels formed the outer skin of the building in the shape of a giant fascia curving over at the top to disguise the junction with the flat roof behind.

The completed Fred Olsen Passenger Terminal rounding the corner of a cargo transit shed.

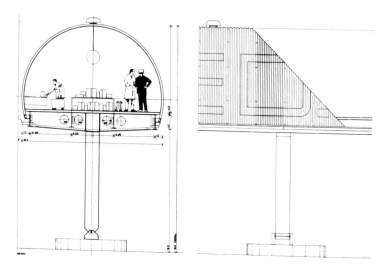

Detailed section and partial elevation.

Cutaway axonometric of the Fred
Olsen passenger terminal.

Following pages: the dockside
elevation of Fred Olsen Operations
and Amenity Centre with reflection
of cargo ship.

While the temporary air structure for Computer Technology still represents the highest level of structural ephemeralization attained by Foster, one of the two permanent buildings erected between 1968 and 1970 for the Fred Olsen shipping line comes a close second. At Millwall Dock in London, the architect designed a passenger terminal for cruise ships that took the form of a 60-meter metal deck supported by steel beams raised above quay level to permit the operation of cargo-loading forklifts. The original design called for a rigid monocoque tube made of two skins of plastic-coated steel, a cladding material like that used at Reliance Controls, to sit above the floor deck. The two skins were to have been cold-rolled to a profiled section off-site and then fixed back-to-back, to maintain the necessary rigidity. However, the monocoque method was discarded for cost reasons, and a single ribbed-aluminum skin was employed, supported by a light-weight steel frame. Natural light was provided by fully glazing each end of the tube as well as by inserting ribbed transparent inserts in the walls.

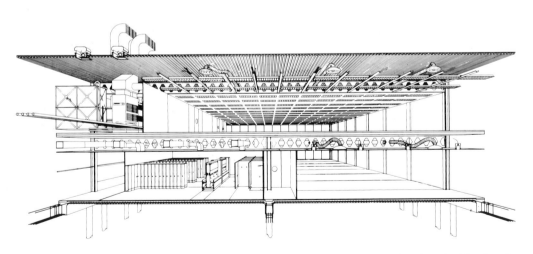

Perspective section of Operations and
Amenity Centre showing service zones.

Opposite page: aerial view, showing Operations and Amenity Centre sandwiched between two cargo transit sheds and the passenger terminal wrapped around one corner of the sheds.

The first building of the Olsen commission, the Amenity Centre, completed in 1969, was a more substantial structure. As with the Computer Technology projects, the Foster office conducted an intensive study of the client's needs. There were two fixed elements at Olsen's Millwall docks, a pair of large cargo transit sheds, each over 16,000 square meters, standing side-by-side with a statutory eight-hour fire separation between them. While the raised passenger terminal was to wrap around the corner of one shed, it seemed that what was originally planned as two separate buildings for operations and amenities would have to be sited away from the quay altogether. But the architects determined that by erecting four-hour fire walls between the two sheds, a two-story building containing both functions could safely be built in the gap. This would bring office and dock workers together in the same space—a radical concept at the time.

Although a story taller and air-conditioned, in its structure, servicing, and space planning the Olsen Amenity Centre was a close cousin to the Computer Technology Research and Development Centre. It used the same steel frame and castellated beam construction and the same roof service zone, although in this case services were hidden by a suspended ceiling and converted into a service 'sandwich zone' at the first-floor level. The principal difference between the buildings involved the glass cladding of the front and rear walls. At Olsen, a neoprene-gasket glazing system was used, the glass stretching from one side of the building to the other and extending vertically from ground level to a discreet capping beam cantilevered from the flange of the highest roof beam. This was the first fully glazed facade in Britain to use high-performance heat and light reflecting glass. During the day, each elevation reflected the outside scene; at night the walls became transparent, exposing the whole interior, including the open edges of the two service zones with their pipes and ventilation ducts. A single, central air-conditioning system was contained within the building; only the compressors and vents penetrated the roof. Inside, the Amenity Centre offered unprecedented high quality facilities for the Olsen workers.

When Fred Olsen Lines left London in the late 1970s, the Amenity Centre became the offices of the London Docklands Development Corporation. It has since been demolished.

Computer Technology
Principal consultants: Anthony Hunt Associates, structural engineers; G.N. Haden & Sons, service engineers
Fred Olsen Lines
Principal consultants: Anthony Hunt Associates, structural engineers; G.N. Haden & Sons, service engineers; Hanscomb Partnership, cost consultants

Tinted glass southern elevation.

Norman Foster: A Global Architecture

IBM Pilot Head Office
Cosham, England, 1970-72

IBM Technical Park
Greenford, England, 1978

The IBM Pilot Head Office at Cosham in Hampshire and the IBM Technical Park, built later at Greenford in Middlesex, complete a cycle begun in 1966 with the 'lost vernacular' of Reliance Controls.

IBM Northern Road, as the Pilot Head Office came to be called, is a discreet single-story structure hidden behind avenues of trees on a spacious site. It began as something else entirely, a proposal for a cluster of temporary buildings that would house 750 IBM staff being relocated out of London. This plan was transformed into an architectural commission because Foster Associates convinced IBM that a new, purpose-designed office would be better and cheaper than a group of temporary, off-the-peg buildings.

Foster Associates proposed a single-story, glass-clad, deep-plan, air-conditioned building with no courtyards or lightwells, which meant that some workstations would be as far as 30 meters from a window. At the time this stretched the dependence on artificial light and air to the limit, but IBM was persuaded that the project was a reasonable short-term solution. Although the building was originally intended to be used for only three to four years, it has proved so successful that, after an extensive refurbishment by Foster Associates in 1987, it will continue to be used into the next century.

In its original form, Northern Road was an 11,000-square-meter rectangular volume with two off-center service cores separated from the bulk of the office space by a wide mall running the building's length; 6,000 square meters of offices to the south of this mall were separated into bays by seven 'fingers' of partially glazed executive offices. To accommodate this arrangement, Foster Associates and structural engineer Anthony Hunt adopted a 7-by-7-meter structural

The perimeter zone used as a corridor.

Exploded plan

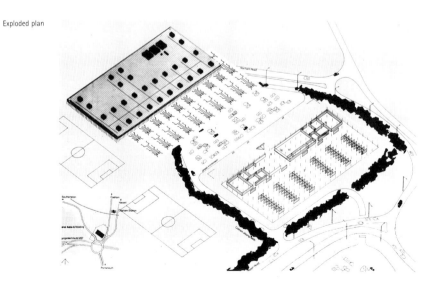

Norman Foster: A Global Architecture

grid composed of square-tube columns supporting lightweight bolted-steel lattice roof beams. The structure's perimeter was enclosed by an aluminum box-section glazing frame with full-height Pilkington Spectrafloat single glazing mounted in neoprene gaskets. Similar to the cladding used at the Fred Olsen Amenity Centre, this arrangement produced a very thin eaves and no expressed structure on the exterior. The system eventually led to the frame-free glazing system used at Willis Faber and Dumas, and the Renault Distribution Center and became a commercial catalog item.

The two service cores provided departure points for heating, cooling, and electrical service distribution, including the circulation of chilled and heated water, which was pumped to roof-mounted air-conditioning units serving groups of 50-square-meter bays. Because the floor was the concrete foundation slab—Northern Road was one of the first non-industrial buildings in Britain to use an American-style power-floated slab—there was no ground-level service distribution except in the mainframe computer room, one of the earliest to be included in an office building, where a raised computer floor was installed with ramp access from the floor outside. Outside of the computer room, all cable and duct distribution took place in an omnidirectional, two-foot service zone between the roof and the suspended ceiling. This space, the edge of which is visible through the perimeter glazing, also served as the air-conditioning system's return-air plenum.

Perspective section showing servicing through roof space.

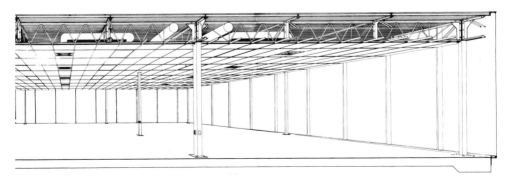

Exterior view, at left, and detail of the exterior cladding, at right, of the IBM Pilot Head office.

Major envelope replacement and space-planning changes at Northern Road occurred in 1985, when full-scale refurbishment for the year 2000 was authorized. The roof covering—felt on insulated profiled-steel decking—was completely replaced because it had reached the end of its useful life. At the same time, the interior was repainted and recarpeted (from wool-nylon to full nylon) and, more significantly, recabled to accommodate a 600-workstation local area network. At Foster Associates' suggestion, this work was coupled with the creation of a foot-high ledge above the cable tracks for employees to display personal items, and a color change from the original browns to blues to match IBM's corporate color scheme.

Three years after the completion of Northern Road, IBM again commissioned Foster Associates to design a new building, this time a distribution center for a West London site at Greenford. As at Cosham, the company had already made its own assessment and favored a design-and-build solution. Foster Associates was invited to try to produce a better solution within the same budget.

The forty-acre Greenford site, bounded by a canal and only four miles from Heathrow Airport, had been left in poor condition by its previous industrial uses. But it offered considerable opportunities. Foster Associates proposed creating a large landscaped area around a double-height distribution center with mezzanine levels. This building eventually expanded to bridge a proposed east-west axis

Interior of perimeter corridor.

road, linking up with a second building, a demonstration and sales center for mainframe computers.

Foster's office initially proposed using temporary inflatables, as at Computer Technology, to provide short-term facilities during construction. The project brief soon changed, though, and the scheme was refined into an elegant two-part structure linked by a habitable bridge (and footbridge below), with a single continuous roofline running from the smaller computer sales building across the east-west access route to the 13,000-square-meter distribution center. The building's steel-frame structural system followed the principles established at Northern Road, though on a much larger scale, with stanchions supporting long-span lattice beams forming service zones. The distribution center was principally clad in ribbed-aluminum sheet with full-height glazed sections, the glazing frames supported

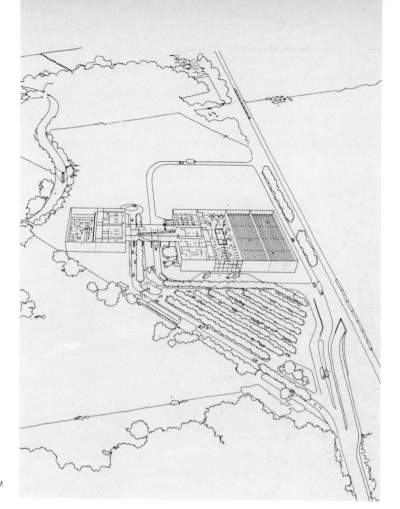

Aerial perspective sketch of the IBM
Greenford building without roof.

Elevation and section showing bridge.

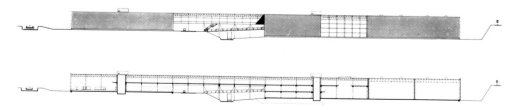

by pierced web steel mullions. The bridge offices and the demonstration and computer sales building have floor-to-ceiling neoprene-gasket glazing based on the technique used for the Fred Olsen Amenity Centre, and the computer building is fitted throughout with a raised floor system, as introduced at Northern Road.

As the photographs show, IBM Greenford achieves something close to the perfect transparency—philosophical as well as literal—that lies at the heart of all great modern architecture. Even the edges of its computer floors are clear glass. And though it's seldom illustrated in anthologies of his work, in many ways the IBM complex at Greenford represents the culmination of Norman Foster's 'universal building' period, which began with the large multifunctional space and overhead servicing at Reliance Controls. Computer Technology, the Fred Olsen buildings, IBM Cosham, and IBM Greenford all stem from this vision of steel-framed, multifunctional space, which in the decade stretching from 1967 to 1978 was used for numerous warehouse, office, retail, and entertainment clients. All of this work comes together at IBM Greenford in a demonstration of what lucid thinking about structure, servicing, and quality of life can contribute to a democratic architecture of the workplace.

IBM Pilot Head Office
Principal consultants (original construction): Anthony Hunt Associates, structural engineers; R.S. Wilcox Associates, service engineers; Hanscomb Partnership, cost consultants
IBM Technical Park
Principal consultants: Anthony Hunt Associates, structural engineers; Northcroft Neighbour & Nicholson, cost consultants; Michael Brown Associates, landscaping

Typical sections.

| Computer room | Core zone | Offices | Offices over car access road | Bridges and low-level truck service road |

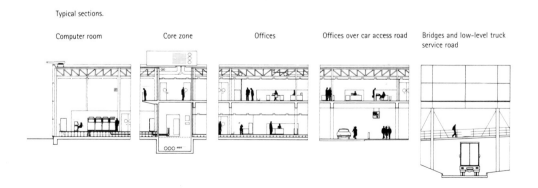

The junction of the bridge building with the Installation
Support Center at night.

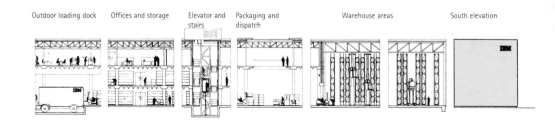

| Outdoor loading dock | Offices and storage | Elevator and stairs | Packaging and dispatch | Warehouse areas | | South elevation |

Willis Faber and Dumas Headquarters
Ipswich, England, 1975

Though clearly descended from the IBM and Fred Olsen projects, the 21,000-square-meter Willis Faber and Dumas building in Ipswich wrought such definitive changes in the elements of the 'lost vernacular' begun with Reliance Controls that it amounts to a new paradigm in itself. It stands as second only to the Hongkong and Shanghai Bank as the definitive achievement of Foster's career.

Looking back at a distance of twenty years, Foster recalled the building's breakthroughs: "Willis Faber and Dumas challenged the typical speculative office building of the period in almost every way. It was an irregular-shaped, low-rise, large-floor-plate urban building when most office buildings were square, small-floor-plate towers; it was air conditioned at a time when most offices in England still weren't; it had a long-span structural grid and a deep plan, instead of a short-span grid and a shallow plan; it used six escalators to communicate between floors where the conventional

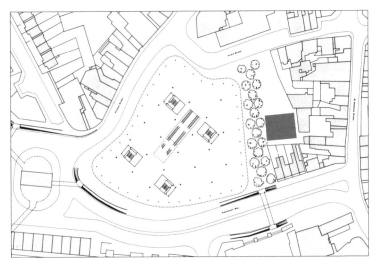

The site plan, below left, shows how the amoeboid perimeter locks into the medieval street plan.

Below, the building transparent at night . . .

... becomes opaque and reflective in daylight.

Norman Foster: A Global Architecture

The main escalator arrives at the roof level.

three-story office of the time would have made do with stairs; it had raised floors for cabling and suspended ceilings for air conditioning; it had a huge lightwell, which would nowadays be called an atrium; it had a roof garden when such things were confined to expensive private houses; and an Olympic-sized swimming pool for the staff. . . . All these innovations were a tremendous success, and in many ways they anticipated the information revolution that was still a decade away. By the time we were commissioned to design another office building, this time for developers, many years later, we found that all the so-called revolutionary features from Ipswich had become the conventional wisdom of office design for tenanted and owner-occupied buildings alike."

Aside from the innovative features Foster enumerates above, this building is best known for its remarkable exploitation of its amoeba-shaped site, dictated by Ipswich's medieval street pattern. The perimeter of the building is ringed with off-grid reinforced-concrete columns linked to the interior by a concrete waffle slab at each floor level. Outside the perimeter of the floor slabs, the building is entirely enclosed in bronzed glass, which is opaque and reflective in daytime and transparent at night, when it exposes a view of the offices. The night view makes it clear that, as a result of the unusual shape of the building, the detailing of the

View up into atrium from entrance.

Opposite page, top: cutaway axonometric through atrium, shown in section below.

Below, left to right: plans at ground, first, second, and roof levels.

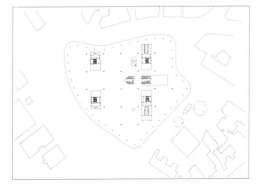

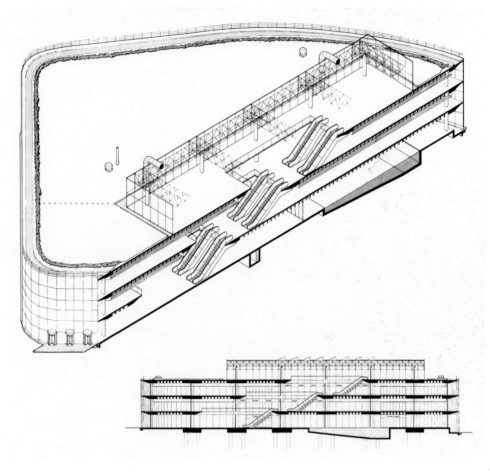

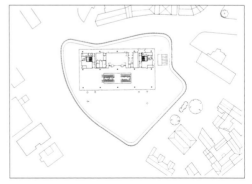

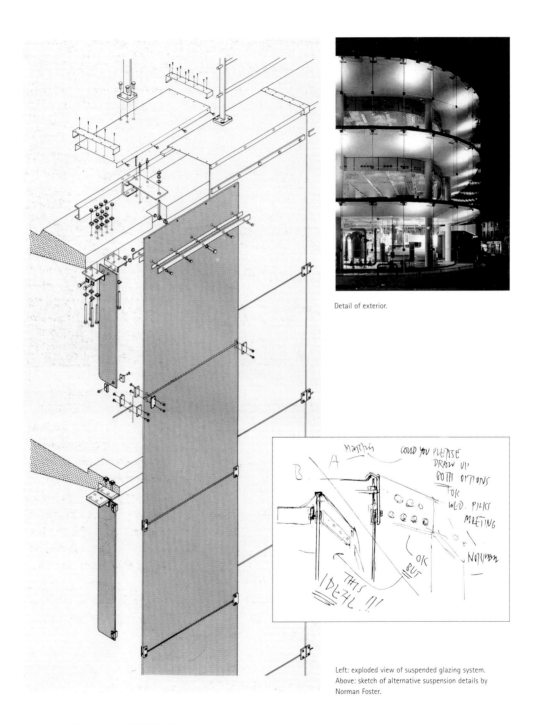

Detail of exterior.

Left: exploded view of suspended glazing system.
Above: sketch of alternative suspension details by
Norman Foster.

View from rooftop restaurant to
roof garden.

interior is more complex and was more difficult to integrate than that of its rectangular predecessors. The edges of the service zones, for example, are neither exposed nor concealed by a false ceiling. Instead, the tapered edges of the floor slab provide the link between the false ceiling and the perimeter of the building.

The building's all-glass facade was a design and engineering achievement of the highest order, especially considering the state of the technology at the time. The glass wall is suspended the full height of the building in two-meter-wide facets, each of which is made up of six panels, suspended from a single bolt on the edge of the roof slab. Vertical connections are made by metal patches that link the corners of four sheets of glass. There are no rigid lateral connections; the glass is allowed to move vertically, restrained by near-invisible, half-story-high glass stiffening fins and sealed with flexible silicon.

In recognition of its innovative design, the Willis Faber and Dumas building is listed by the Department of the Environment as being of unique architectural interest and importance.

Principal consultants: Anthony Hunt Associates, structural engineers; John Taylor & Sons, civil engineers; Davis Belfield & Everest, cost consultants

Sainsbury Centre for Visual Arts and Crescent Wing

University of East Anglia, Norwich, England, 1977/1991

Sketch by Norman Foster.

If the Willis Faber and Dumas building represents the culmination of ten years of development of the postindustrial workplace, the Sainsbury Centre for Visual Arts at the University of East Anglia symbolizes a dramatic invasion of the world of academic architecture by a form of construction previously thought appropriate only for military or aerospace buildings. Designed as a home for the Sainsbury Collection of ethnic and European art, presented as a gift to the university in 1973, the dramatic and uncompromising building is a product of the unusual rapport that grew between the architect and his patrons, the collectors and donors Sir Robert and Lady Sainsbury. Freedom from commercial constraints and the trust between architect and client enabled Foster to refine the design to a very high degree.

The Sainsbury Centre for Visual Arts is a 130-by-30-by-7.5-meter rectangular box, articulated inside by an elevator and two minor mezzanines that loosely divide the space into separate areas without interfering with the ability to see from one end to the

Main exhibition space.

other. At one end of the rectangle is a restaurant; next to it are offices and tutorial rooms around an internal courtyard, the heart of the School of Fine Arts; then the main gallery, and finally the reception and temporary exhibition areas.

These facilities are enclosed by a series of tubular steel portal frames of unique 'hollow wall' design—the space between the inner and outer chords of the diagonally braced trusses is utilized as part of the facility, contributing to the clarity of the plan. The 2.4-meter space between the inner and outer skins of the hollow walls is wide enough to accommodate all the building's services and lighting-control equipment as well as toilets, cloakrooms, storage, and a darkroom, allowing the building to take on the form of a pure inverted U, rectangular in plan as well as elevation and seemingly connected to the university's walkway system only by a slender elevated pedestrian bridge that enters at a high level. (There are, in fact, ground-level entrances and vehicular access in the basement.)

Cutaway showing superstructure
and basement vehicle access.

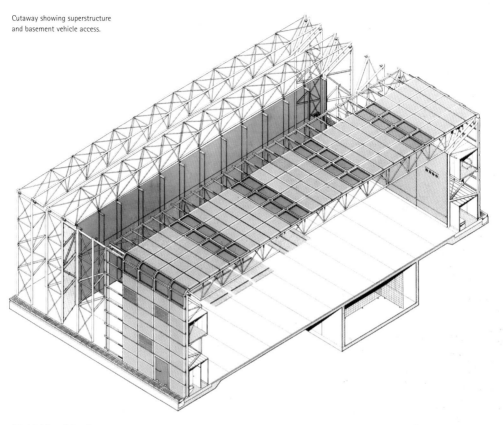

Spiral stair from high walkway.

Rear service entrance ramp.

Aerial view of Sainsbury Centre before the addition of Crescent Wing.

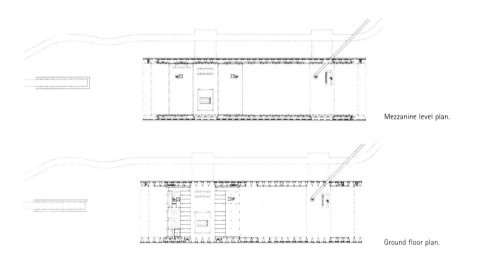

Mezzanine level plan.

Ground floor plan.

The hollow-wall and roof-space areas are enclosed on the exterior by a plastic-coated aluminum-panel system, and on the inside by adjustable louvers. Because the external aluminum panels are interchangeable with the glass panels that form the long series of overhead skylights, and because the overhead and lateral louvers can be adjusted from the space between the two skins, it is possible to adjust the whole exhibition environment without disturbing the interior. Each end of the inverted-U shape is fully glazed, while the tubular steel skeleton of the 'hollow' wall itself is exposed beyond the line of the glazing, where it includes additional strut bracing that stiffens the entire structure. Appropriate for a building using what were then very advanced techniques in aluminum, steel, glass, and neoprene, its performance in relation to its weight remains impressive. With a floor area of some 6,500 square meters, the structure and cladding weigh only just over 5,000 tons—4,000 tons of which is made up of the concrete substructure.

The completion of this remarkable building in 1977 so soon after the critical success of the Willis Faber and Dumas building established Norman Foster at the head of the triumvirate of leading British architects: himself, Richard Rogers, and James Stirling. Within one year, the Sainsbury Centre had received the Reynolds Aluminum Award, the Museum of the Year Award, and the Royal Institute of British Architects' Building of the Year Award. It picked up many other honors in the years following, culminating in Norman Foster's receipt of the RIBA Gold Medal in 1983.

Long section showing hydraulic elevators.

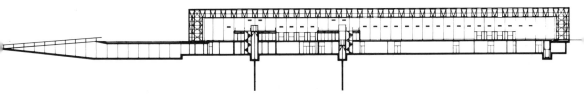

In 1986 Sir Robert and Lady Sainsbury returned to the university and offered a further donation for a facility that would house their reserve collection as well as accommodate conferences, temporary exhibitions, offices, and conservation workshops. It was assumed at first that the original Sainsbury building would simply be extended—it is, after all, a linear structure on a site that permits expansion to the southeast—but sentiment opposed this. The building had entered the popular imagination a decade before as a complete and perfect object, and it was thought that an extension would diminish this.

Foster's office proposed extending the building underground, creating a 3,300-square-meter top-lit extension to the basement of the main building. This scheme involved building new subterranean facilities along the projected line of the original building, but terminating its rectangular geometry with a wide, curving corridor marked by continuous white-fritted glazing flush with the downward slope of the land towards the lake to the southeast. The curve of this glazing gave the new extension its name, the Crescent Wing. Statutory regulations requiring guardrails above the sloping glazing and projecting roof lights caused only a minor disturbance to the Sainsbury Centre's original appearance. The addition increased the center's utility and added 50 percent more floor space.

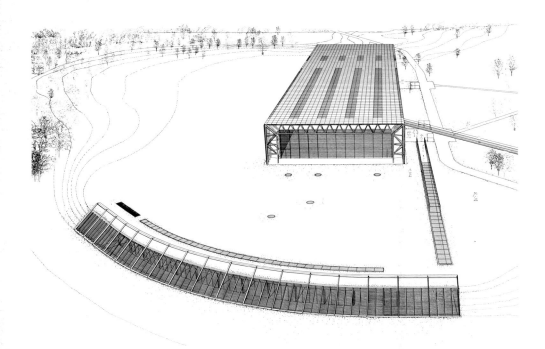

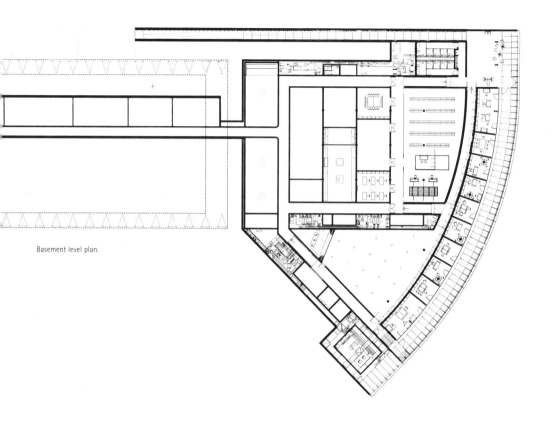

Basement level plan.

The glazed corridor at night.

The study reserve collection.

Sainsbury Centre for Visual Arts
Principal consultants: Anthony Hunt Associates, structural engineers; John Taylor
& Son, civil engineers; Davis Belfield & Everest, cost consultant
Crescent Wing
Principal consultants: YRM Anthony Hunt Associates, structural engineers;
J. Roger Preston & Partners, service engineers; Henry Riley & Son, cost consultants

Interior view of entrance and
reception area and, following pages,
general view with entrance canopy
in foreground.

Renault Distribution Centre
Swindon, England, 1982

Built on a sixteen-acre site in a business park on the outskirts of Swindon, only a mile or so from the Reliance Controls factory, this 27,000-square-meter parts distribution center was commissioned by the French car manufacturer Renault as its main warehousing facility in the United Kingdom.

A return to industrial architecture after some years of concentrating on commercial buildings, this project gave Foster Associates an opportunity to further refine the performance and utility of its long-span steel-frame design by introducing mast-supported trusses to create even larger unobstructed floor spaces. The result is a building that consists largely of its own elaborate roofing system, which itself is an interesting precursor to the spectacular roof later designed for the passenger terminal at Stansted Airport.

The building's structure is based on a modular system of suspended roof sections supported by tubular steel masts 16 meters high and 24 meters apart. These masts are connected by trusses that combine convex perforated web steel beams in compression with concave tensile-steel rods in tension. This primary structure is painted bright yellow inside and out and is clearly visible around the perimeter

Elevation detail.

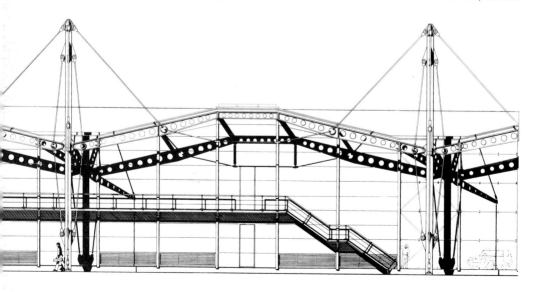

South elevation.

Section through offices, training
areas, and showroom.

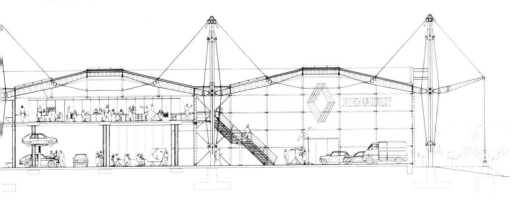

of the building, where the final row of masts on each side is outrigged from the building envelope and ground-anchored, creating a sharp contrast with the windowless gray metal cladding of the warehouse area and the glazed non-warehouse areas. Truss penetration through the side walls is made possible by the use of a flexible neoprene eaves. The roof covering above the undulating metal decking is formed from a single site-welded skin of reinforced PVC that is penetrated by the suspension masts and rods as well as by large skylights.

The plan of the distribution center is simple, consisting of four parallel rows of 24-meter modules for warehousing replacement parts. Non-warehouse facilities are housed in six staggered modules to the right of the entrance. These comprise a fully glazed single module that serves as a vehicle showroom, a double module that includes an entrance canopy and restaurant, and a triple module incorporating training and workshop areas.

Upon its completion in 1982 the distribution center was featured in several advertising campaigns for Renault.

Principal consultants: Ove Arup & Partners, structural engineers; Davis Belfield & Everest, cost consultants; Quickborner Team, office planning

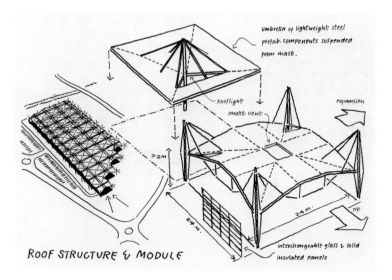

Drawing showing how basic roof module multiplies to form building.

ROOF STRUCTURE & MODULE

Hongkong and Shanghai Bank Headquarters
Hong Kong, China, 1986

Century Tower
Tokyo, Japan, 1991

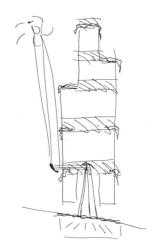

Standing in the heart of Hong Kong's central business district, the 180-meter-tall Hongkong and Shanghai Bank Headquarters tower represented a powerful expression of confidence in the future of the British colony when the tower opened in 1986, eleven years before the territory reverted to Chinese rule. Foster Associates won an international competition to design the building in 1979. Working from its base in London and a new office in Hong Kong, the firm met the bank's brief to build 'the best bank headquarters in the world.'

From the outset the architects departed from the conventions of the commercial high rise, dispensing with a central structural core incorporating elevator shafts and stairs. Instead, the building is divided into three vertically distinct bays of different heights—thirty-five, forty-seven, and twenty-eight stories. Within each bay, floors are suspended from 'bridges' linking large masts located on either side of the building to create a combined office tower with 99,000 square meters of floor space offering excellent views from all work stations and unrivalled operational flexibility. The steel masts are linked by five suspension trusses. Acting (and constructed) like suspension bridges, each of these double-height trusses supports the weight of the eight reinforced-concrete floors immediately below. They also serve as terraces and fire refuges, and they counterbalance the central floor load with the apparent weight of the prefabricated service modules, risers, and stairs located outside of the vertical pylons. At the competition stage, this radical approach enabled the architects to retain the old banking hall during construction, a demand of the client's which was later relaxed. The long-span trusses are clearly expressed on the building's exterior, the structural steel-work itself is concealed but also visually strengthened by close-fitting aluminum cladding.

The Hongkong and Shanghai Bank with the original Bank of China in the foreground.

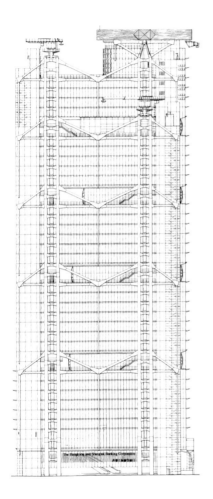

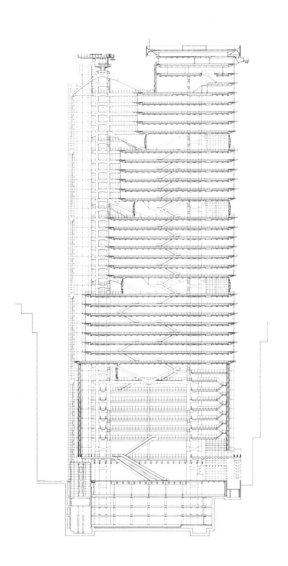

North elevation and section showing
division of building into structural zones.

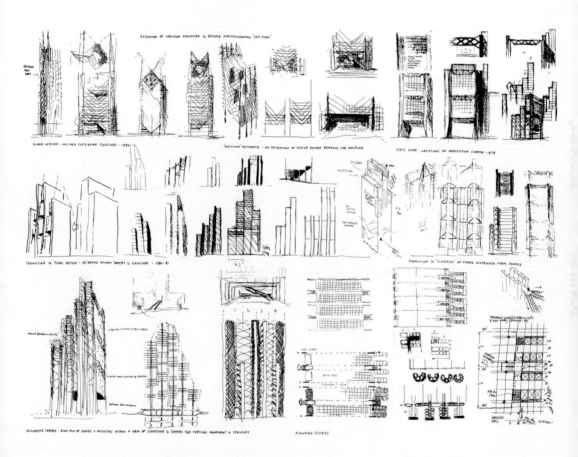

EXTENSION OF CHEVRON STRUCTURE TO BECOME ELECTROGRAPHIC 'SKY SIGN'

SECOND VERSION - INCLINED SUSPENSION STRUCTURE - 1980

'GATEWAY' ENTRANCE - AN EXTENSION OF STATUE SQUARE BENEATH THE BUILDING

FIRST STAGE - VARIATIONS OF COMPETITION SCHEME - 1979

TRANSITION TO FINAL DESIGN - ENTRANCE WITHIN TOWERS & STRUCTURE - 1980-81

TRANSITION TO 'CLUSTERS' OF FLOORS SUSPENDED FROM TOWERS

RECURRING THEMES - RICH MIX OF SPACES & ACTIVITIES WITHIN A GRID OF STRUCTURE & TOWERS FOR VERTICAL MOVEMENT & SERVICES

PLANNING STUDIES

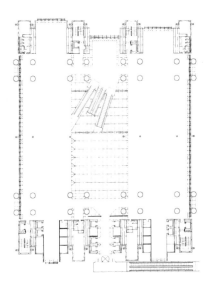 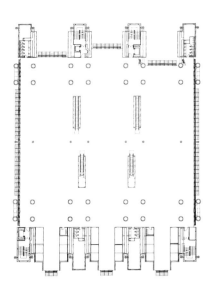

Level three / banking hall plan and typical three-bay-level plan.

Opposite page: view of atrium looking toward elevator lobbies.

The absence of any obvious load-bearing structures between the widely separated pylons creates the distinctive appearance of the building as well as the large column-free areas inside, which allow a very flexible internal organization. The construction also facilitates the suspension of the whole central section of the building over an open, street-level pedestrian plaza. From this plaza, visitors enter the banking hall above by way of obliquely angled escalators that penetrate a curved glazed ceiling. Above the banking hall is the building's most dramatic internal feature, a soaring 52-meter-high atrium that reaches up through ten stories to the inner reflecting mirror of the building's 'sun scoop,' a computer-controlled array of mirrors that adjusts to the solar calendar and reflects light into the atrium and down through the glass ceiling to the plaza below.

The building is clad in silver-gray aluminum painted to automotive standards, and sealed, double-glazed, full-height glass panels. To ensure the highest standards of workmanship, most of the building's components were fabricated in other locations and shipped to Hong Kong for final assembly. The first phase of the building was completed in July 1985.

The Hongkong and Shanghai Bank attracted numerous awards, notably the 1986 Premier Award of the Royal Academy of Arts, the 1986 Institution of Structural Engineers Special Award, and the 1988 Quaternario Award for Innovative Technology in Architecture.

Commissioned shortly after the completion of the Hongkong and Shanghai Bank, Century Tower is an adaptation of some of that building's revolutionary structure to Tokyo's speculative office market. Designed for the Obunsha Publishing Group by Foster Associates' London office and a new project office opened in Tokyo, the 28,000-square-meter development consists of two linked towers nineteen and twenty stories high separated by a full-height atrium. This brings daylight into the center of the building on all floors, without a complex arrangement like the Hong Kong 'sun scoop.' The ground and basement levels accommodate a restaurant, tea house, art gallery, pools, and health club.

In the towers themselves the office floors are arranged in double-height units

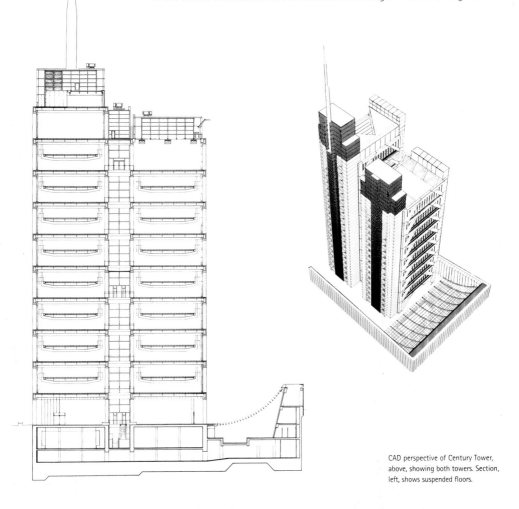

CAD perspective of Century Tower, above, showing both towers. Section, left, shows suspended floors.

Office spaces showing suspended
floors.

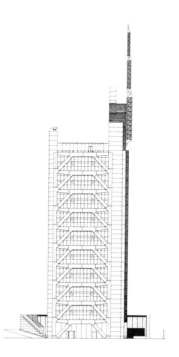

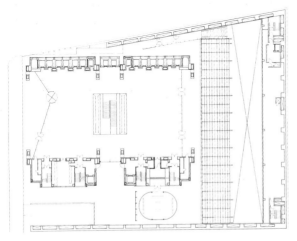

South elevation, above, and level
one plan.

each with a suspended mezzanine—a smaller version of the suspension system used in Hong Kong, but using the same principle of long-span, bridgelike structures between combined supports and service zones to avoid a floor space-sapping central core. As in Hong Kong, this structure is clearly expressed on the exterior of the building; the twin towers reveal the absence of supports in the central office floor areas as well as the presence of the diagonal bracing required by stringent fire and earthquake codes.

Hongkong and Shanghai Bank
Principal consultants: Ove Arup & Partners, structural engineers; J. Roger Preston & Partners, service engineers; Levett & Bailey and Northcroft Neighbour & Nicholson, cost consultants; Claude R. Engle, lighting
Century Tower
Principal consultants: Ove Arup & Partners, structural engineers; J. Roger Preston & Partners, service engineers; Northcroft Neighbour & Nicholson, cost consultants

Nomos Furniture System
1985

The first office furniture Foster designed for a client was for Computer Technology in the early 1970s. Ten years later, the architects designed an adjustable cast- and tubular-aluminum drafting table for their new offices in London's Great Portland Street; no existing product was flexible enough for their needs. Soon after that, Renault requested modified versions of these tables for the reception areas and staff restaurant at its parts distribution center in Swindon. This was the origin of the Nomos range of furniture—the name means 'fair distribution' in Greek.

The Nomos system is based on close observation of ergonomic demands in the workplace and on the design of a group of precision components that can be arranged to create workstations for individuals or groups. The starting point of the system is a spine with a vertebra-like conduit, to which are added legs, feet, supports, work surfaces, superstructures, and lighting. These installations can grow to an almost unlimited extent, accommodating shelves, cabling, computers, storage, and sign systems for both sitting and standing work.

Nomos has been in production since 1986. It won both the Stuttgart Design Center Award and the Premio Compasso d'Oro award in its first year.

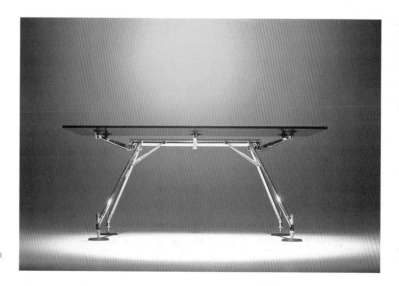

Front and end-on views of a typical Nomos desk.

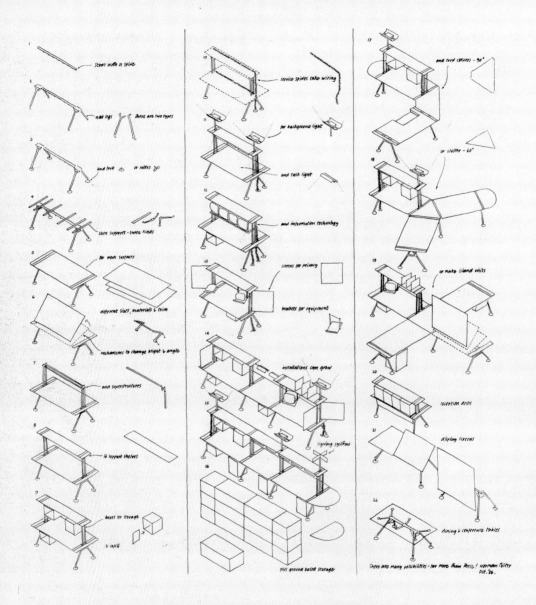

1 start with a spine

2 add legs   there are two types

3 and feet   or rollers

4 then supports - three kinds

5 for work surfaces

6 different sizes, materials & trim

   mechanisms to change height & angle

7 and superstructures

8 to support shelves

9 boxes for storage

   & infill

10 service spines take wiring

11 for background light

    and task light

12 and information technology

13 screens for privacy

    brackets for equipment

14 installations can grow

15 signing systems

16 plus ground based storage

17 and turn corners - 90°

    or cluster - 60°

18

19 or make island units

20 reception desks

21 display screens

22 dining & conference tables

There are many possibilities - far more than these! Norman Foster
Oct. '86.

One of the many configurations possible
with the Nomos system, more of which
are shown sketched by Norman Foster
on the opposite page.

Opposite page: Norman Foster and colleagues
during one of their discussions with Buckminster Fuller about the Samuel Beckett Theatre.
Below: a model of the Autonomous House.

Projects with Richard Buckminster Fuller
1971–83

Norman Foster was an admirer of Richard Buckminster Fuller over a long period and collaborated with him on a number of projects. Like many idealistic architects of his generation, Foster fully accepted Fuller's dictum that the overall purpose of architectural design was to continually achieve higher and higher standards of living at a lower and lower cost in energy and resources. In 1983, only ten days before his death, Fuller, an RIBA Royal Gold Medalist himself, delivered the oration on the occasion of Norman Foster's receiving that honor.

Their first collaboration was the design of the Samuel Beckett Theatre, a radical project for an auditorium in a geodesic capsule buried beneath the quadrangle of St. Peter's College, Oxford. Fuller likened the theater to a nuclear submarine. The location was chosen to make it possible to occupy a central site in an otherwise built-up area. Although the project failed to attract enough funding, their preliminary design work included an early exploration of underground structures—notably, developing methods to resist their tendency to float upward—that was to inform later projects.

Model of house showing twin
concentric domes.

Six years later, Fuller and Foster collaborated on the design of the theme pavilion for the International Energy Expo, to be held in Knoxville, Tennessee in 1982.
They proposed a large, lozenge-shaped double-skin 'tensegrity' structure that
would house the entire exhibition. The climate-controlled enclosure would be
large enough to serve the community as a public building after the exhibition. A
refinement of an earlier structure by Fuller, the United States Pavilion for Expo '67
in Montreal, the Knoxville project would have included within its double skin a
wide range of solar heating, cooling, and electricity-generating devices to maintain comfortable conditions at all times. This project, too, failed to attract funding
and was abandoned after preliminary studies.

Fuller and Foster's final collaboration cast the former in the role of client and
the latter as architect. The project was for a house embodying some of Fuller's

Buckminster Fuller's 'Fly's eye
dome' of 1965, a precursor to the
Foster house.

structural ideas; it was to take the form of a double-skin truncated sphere 15
meters in diameter. The two skins were to revolve independently of one another,
running in low-friction hydraulic races, so little effort would be required to move
them. Since part of each skin was opaque and part transparent, the house could
be darkened or lightened by rotation. The inner skin of the dome supported the
intermediate floors, so in the same way it could reorientate the interior to suit the
position of the sun, the direction of the wind, or other factors.

A large-scale model of this structure was made in the design studio of a U.S.
aircraft manufacturer, then brought to London and reassembled in Foster Associates' office. Detailed design work continued until Fuller's death in the summer
of 1983. Fuller & Sadao Inc. worked as structural consultant for the house
project.

Carré d'Art
Nîmes, France, 1993

Cranfield University Library
Bedfordshire, England, 1993

Although the commission to design a 6,000-square-meter combined modern art gallery and public library in Nîmes, France, was originally won by Foster Associates in an international competition in 1984, construction did not begin until 1987. Work was halted the next year by severe flooding, which prompted a partial redesign of the building that raised its ground floor onto a five-foot podium. The building was not completed until 1993, the same year as the library at Cranfield University in southeast England.

While both buildings are uncompromisingly modern in character, the Carré d'Art is the more imposing, its form and proportions drawing on the classic grandeur of its neighbor, the 1,700-year-old Maison Carrée, one of the most perfectly preserved Roman buildings. It is also informed by the vernacular buildings of the Midi, with their shaded courtyards, frequent flights of steps, and open terraces. The building was conceived originally as a nine-story reinforced-concrete structure, clad in white and translucent glass and making extensive use of vertical and horizontal louvers for sun shading. Its service functions are located at its perimeter; public spaces are centralized. Five of its nine stories were to be below ground level, to allow the building to conform to the general height of the surrounding architecture, while the center of the building above ground opens onto a six-story courtyard beneath what was intended to be a retractable roof.

The organization of the building's facilities follows the logic of its circulation, which centers on three parallel stairs with glass treads; the broadest central flight leads from the entrance up to

View of the Carré d'Art through the columns of the Roman Maison Carrée

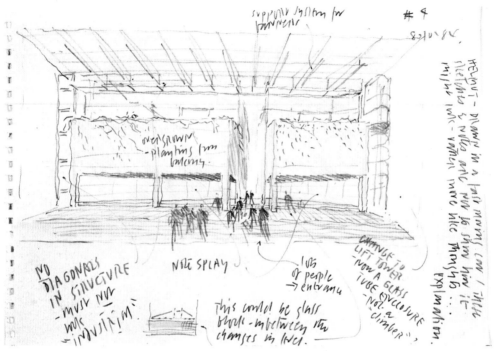

Original sketch and notes for competition scheme by Norman Foster.

Ground level plan.

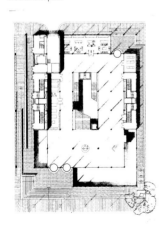

Médiathèque level plan.

Top gallery and café level plan.

The library with
artwork by
Richard Long.

the courtyard. Art galleries occupy the upper floors, making maximum use of filtered daylight. Immediately above and below ground level is the library; meeting rooms, conference facilities, a cinema, and storage are located below ground.

Following the 1988 flood and the raising of the ground floor to podium height, an extra floor and mezzanine were inserted in the basement, increasing the area and height of the whole building. The visual effect of this development was countered by separating the gallery roofs and expressing each individually. At this point, the retractable courtyard roof was replaced by fixed glazing and the site was enlarged to include the square containing the Maison Carrée in front of the building. The use of this square as a gathering place has caused a ripple effect that extends beyond the site via the surrounding streets, which have been restricted to pedestrian traffic to help regenerate the social fabric of the city.

Cranfield University, on the site of an old Royal Air Force base near Milton Keynes, is not located in an ancient city. Indeed, it is a completely artificial place, founded in 1946 as an international center for the study of aeronautics, and since 1969 also serving as a university specializing in management studies. In 1985 Cranfield was given a government grant of $11 million to improve its library. The resulting building has some features in common with the Carré d'Art.

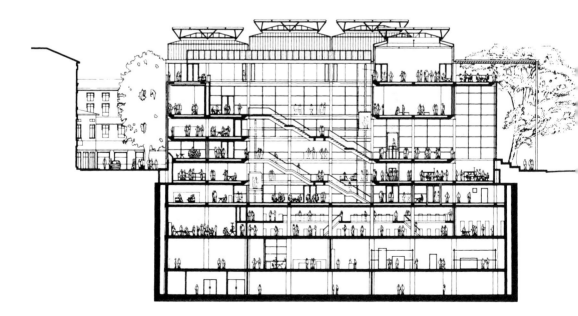

Exterior view of
Carré d'Art.

Long section showing the relationship between
Carré d'Art and the Maison Carrée.

Cranfield Library entrance by night.

With 3,000 square meters spread over three floors, the Cranfield library is less than half the size of the Nîmes building but, in its modest surroundings, it is big enough and elegant enough to transform and impose a sense of order on this part of the Cranfield campus. The exterior of the library is dominated by metal louvers and the projecting ends of four large, glistening barrel vaults. This roof structure is steel-clad and steel-framed, although the rest of the building is of reinforced concrete painted externally, untouched internally, and clad in glass. Like all non-roof-serviced Foster buildings, the experience of the library is as much about the quality of light as the quality of space. All its solar shading devices are positioned outside the building envelope, so that even the roof lights are built up above the apex of the barrel vaults, relying on internal winged baffles to bounce the daylight off the profiled metal ceiling panels.

The lighting of the building from its sides is modulated in different ways. To

First floor library.

Cross section through Cranfield Library.

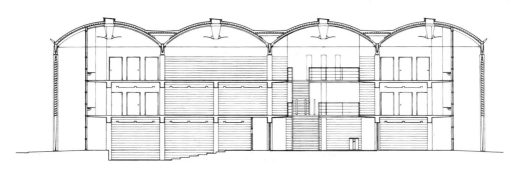

the south, the view out through the entrance to the gray brick-paved square is almost completely clear, because a large projecting roof portico is there to shade the glass. To the east and west, the views from the upper floors of the library are unobstructed but split up into slots by the outrigged metal louvers.

The dominant feature of the library's interior is its stair. With glass treads supported by stainless-steel spreaders on two square-section steel beams, it echoes the form of the broad Nîmes stairs, though on a more modest scale.

Carré d'Art
Principal consultants: Ove Arup & Partners and OTH Mediterranee, consultant engineers; OTH Mechanical, service engineers; Thorne Wheatley Associes., cost consultants
Cranfield University Library
Principal consultants: Ove Arup & Partners, structural engineers; J. Roger Preston & Partners, service engineers; Davis Langdon & Everest, cost consultants

Ground floor plan.

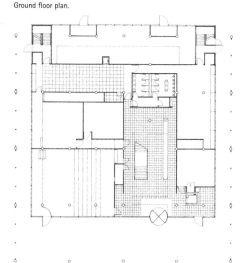

Second floor plan.

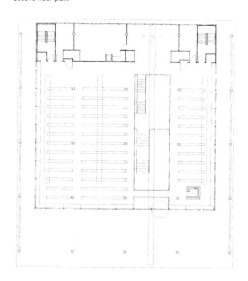

BBC Radio Centre
London, England, 1982

The BBC Radio Centre project marked several firsts for Foster Associates. It was the firm's first major metropolitan commission, the first in which computer-aided design played an important part, and one of the first in which contextual and conservation issues were of great significance.

Although plans for a new central London BBC Radio Centre were abandoned after three years of preparatory work, in some ways the exercise laid the foundation for the adroitness and confidence with which Norman Foster was to approach historical sites and contexts in the future. From the beginning of the BBC saga in May 1982, when the firm won a limited competition to design the building, Foster was determined to show that he could deliver his usual level of advanced technology while rising to the challenge of a historically sensitive urban site.

The firm's brief involved replacing a Victorian hotel already owned by the BBC with a new 54,000-square-meter building facing the network's original 1931 Broadcasting House at an angle across Portland Place. Besides the urban context and conservation issues that were to delay the building until a sudden change of chairman led to its being canceled altogether, there were three principal design issues: the building had to provide surplus cabling and technical capacity to allow

Cavendish Place elevation.

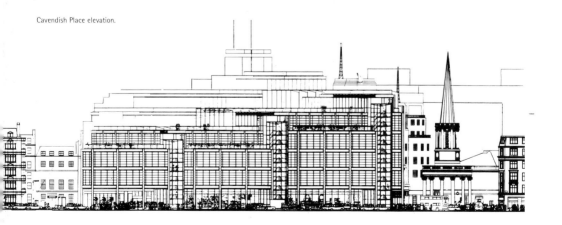

for every foreseeable broadcasting development, construction could not interfere with broadcasting activities, and the center had to replace as many of the BBC's scattered London offices as possible.

In pursuit of a design that could satisfy all these requirements, the Foster team evaluated more than a hundred options, which ranged from demolishing the hotel to converting the site into a park and building elsewhere. The firm soon focused its attention on a three-dimensional planning arrangement that stressed the diagonal axis running across the site from the spire of All Souls Church to the center of Cavendish Square. This motif eventually became a full-length diagonal atrium that would also have served as a public right-of-way, with shops, cafés, and trees. The building was to have been of relatively conventional reinforced-concrete construction with heavy waffle slab floors for acoustic isolation. Radio facilities were

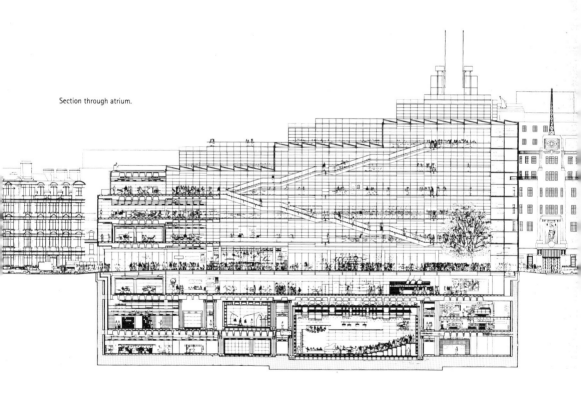

Section through atrium.

placed on either side of the atrium and below it, in three subterranean stories of sound studios and auditoriums.

The final breakthrough concerned the building's massing. When the design was finished, subsidiary skylights at right angles to the diagonal atrium became steps in a roofline that rose from an almost domestic four-story scale on the corner projecting into Cavendish Square to seven stories above the tall glass wall at the end of the atrium facing All Souls Church. In a final refinement reminiscent of the earlier Willis Faber and Dumas building, the firm proposed that the roof be covered with grass and that a rooftop staff restaurant be built.

Just before the scheme was to be submitted for planning permission in 1985, the BBC decided to sell the site and develop a larger one in West London. The Victorian hotel, thus saved from demolition, was refurbished and reopened with some success.

Principal consultants: Ove Arup & Partners, structural engineers; YRM Engineers, service engineers; Davis Belfield & Everest, cost consultants

Sketch and notes by Norman Foster.

Model view through atrium to
All Souls Church.

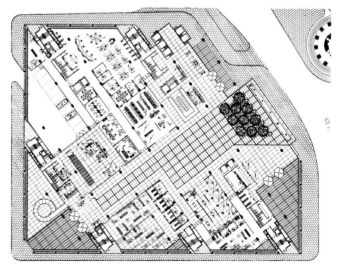

Ground floor plan showing public
"street" through atrium.

ITN Headquarters
London, England, 1990

The headquarters for Independent Television News, built on the former site of a newspaper's offices in Gray's Inn Road, belongs to a new genre of urban contextual buildings by Foster that can be traced back to the BBC Radio Centre. The building's buttoned-down, understated modernism is a response to the strong pressures for conformity that exist in London and other European cities committed to a heritage culture that sees no virtue in new buildings that flaunt their novelty.

The 40,000-square-meter ITN building was preceded by another 'purist' building, Foster Associates' own offices in Battersea, completed in 1990. In both cases, only part of the building was intended to be occupied by the client. This imposed a discipline unusual for an architect whose best work had always been executed for owner-occupier clients untroubled by the fickleness of the real estate market.

The economics of real estate development determine key design parameters on any project. The use of a concrete structural frame at that at Battersea and ITN instead of the steelwork Foster had previously favored is a case in point. And while the eight-story ITN building is considerably larger than that at Battersea, both have the owners' offices at the base and speculative areas above.

The ITN building and the architect's Battersea offices both have a cross section that makes plain the prominence of a double-height floor with a mezzanine related to the ground level, with another floor or floors beneath. In the case of the Battersea building, this deep-plan lower floor is daylit from the front. At ITN it is deeper—30 meters—and more extensive, having originally been a basement housing printing presses. While much of this space was converted to television studios, part of it has been daylit by means of a pierced ground-floor slab that allows the broad atrium above to bring daylight to the lowest level. Both buildings are framed using long-span structural bays with cylindrical columns set back behind glass cladding that requires some kind of treatment to control heat gain and solar glare. At Battersea, fabric blinds are used, while at ITN there is a more elaborate double-glazed facade, with retractable blinds in the cavity between each skin that also acts as an air-conditioning return-air plenum. Both buildings use extensive metal louvers to clad service and elevator shafts.

Interior view of the atrium.

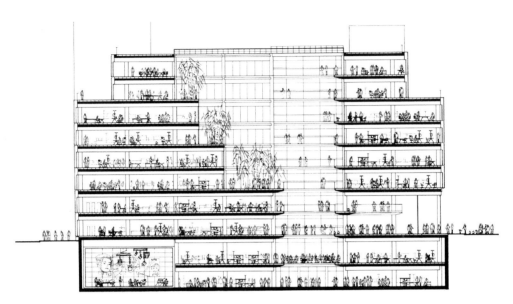

Cross section, east-west

Ground floor plan.   Level three plan.

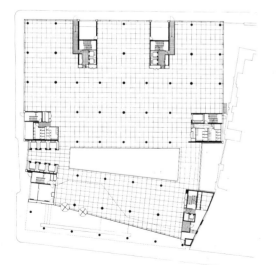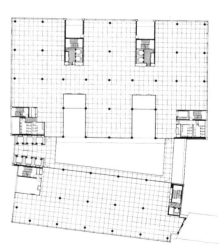

View across atrium to open news-broadcasting studio.

While neatly, even severely detailed, the ITN building's street facade is modest and unobtrusive. Once inside, there is a spectacular atrium, stepping down from the highest level via three floors of heavily planted internal gardens. Circulation between floors is by means of high-speed glass elevators. Everywhere there is the powerful directing effect of Foster's design for the envelope, atrium, and core areas, with its acid-etched and tinted glass, light blue carpets, greenish blinds, and silver anodized aluminum balustrades. Tenants looking at the raised floors and suspended ceilings employed on the parts of the building Foster Associates finished have decided they could do no better than to use the same design themselves. In fact, the only departure from Foster's list of main subcontractors and suppliers has been in the partitioning system; one tenant decided against the original metal system and installed a wood-framed design of their own.

One thing the architects strove to create was the possibility—though security problems prevented it from ever becoming a reality—of an unprecedented interaction between the public and a TV news station, with large video screens enabling visitors to imbibe some of the excitement and immediacy of the world of electronic information.

Principal consultants: Ove Arup & Partners, structural engineers; J. Roger Preston & Partners, service engineers; Davis Belfield & Everest, cost consultants; Sandy Brown Associates, acoustics

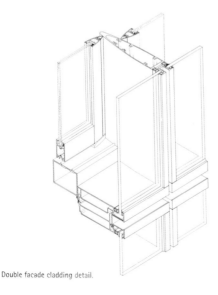

Double facade cladding detail.

Handrail detail.

The studios seen through the cables
of the Albert Bridge and, opposite,
elevation from the river.

Foster and Partners Studios
Battersea, London, England, 1991

The first thing that strikes a visitor to Riverside Three, Norman Foster's London office and home, is the unshakable faith in the ideals of modernism that the building radiates. In a city where modernism is frequently under attack, Bauhaus principles of light, air, cleanness of outline, and structural integrity are alive and well here on the south bank of the Thames. Riverside Three's concrete skeleton, only eight stories high, effortlessly dominates the river between the Battersea and Albert bridges, especially at night, when the immense width of the double-height drawing office is thrown open to the gaze of the Chelsea embankment, revealing a balconied mezzanine of conference rooms and libraries and the vast studio below, buzzing with activity.

This nighttime view is a perfect metaphor for the manner in which the architect approaches the design of interiors. What you see through the glass at Riverside Three is what you get when you visit the building. For Foster, the interior of a building is not a separate or secondary design problem; in shape and material it flows from the supporting and enclosing structure, and from the increasingly elaborate servicing systems that modern buildings require. The materials used for 'interior

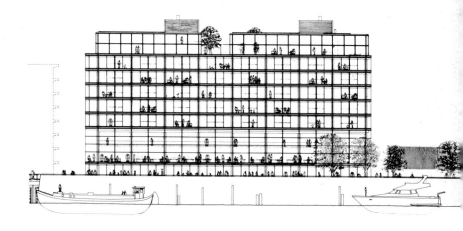

Studios and apartments seen from
across the river.

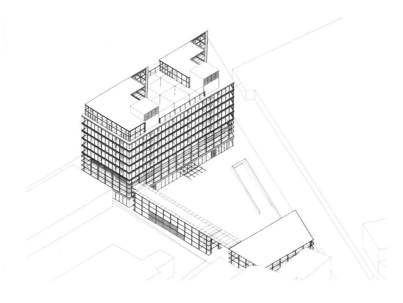

Aerial perspective.

Change in proportions of glazing mark main studio.

design' are the same as the materials used for construction. The only decoration—if indeed it can be called that—is the activity of the building's occupants and the natural and artificial light that illuminates it.

Circumstances required the building to be relatively cheap, yet it contrasts strongly with its surroundings, an area of sheds and warehouses that Foster dismisses tersely as 'Beirut.' Within the curtilage of the site another world opens up. A flight of granite steps set between plain white walls runs 12 meters to a reception area marked by a long Foster-designed Nomos glass table. And while the entrance steps may be a **tour de force,** they do little to prepare one for the spectacular 9,400-cubic-meter space that forms the centerpiece of the building. Seen from inside, the great glazed north wall of the drawing office, like a gigantic windshield, offers an unbroken panoramic view of the Thames. The Battersea and Albert bridges and the traffic on Cheyne Walk seem so near that you could almost reach out and touch them. To either side the unedifying views of 'Beirut' are hidden by close-fitting white fabric blinds. No 'interior design' could ever match the kaleidoscopic detail revealed by this unrestricted view of the outside world. This was the dream of the 'Glass Architecture' of eighty years ago, only now it is executed in gigantic sheets of tinted, low-E, laminated glass.

The studio at Riverside Three is a living example of what Norman Foster means by an interior created by structure, cladding, and activity. It is 60 meters long, 24 meters deep, 6.5 meters high, and entirely glazed on its north side. Looking down from the mezzanine on the southern side of the studio, the tranquility is almost palpable. Below, rolling from east to west over a sea of gray carpet, are thirteen great double-sided drawing tables. At these desks sit partners, architects, assistants, and secretaries—there are no partitioned offices in the studio.

This studio floor is only one of the innovations incorporated into Riverside Three. On the building's south elevation, clear glazing gives way to white enamel fritted glass—using a technique borrowed from the automotive industry and developed for use at Riverside—and more taut white blinds to provide shade.

Principal consultants: Ove Arup & Partners, structural engineers; J. Roger Preston & Partners, service engineers; Schumann Smith, cost consultants; Claude R. Engle, lighting

Section showing dramatic access steps.

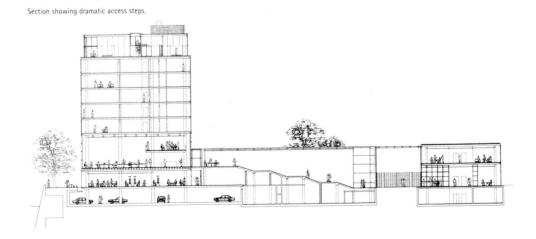

Inside the main studio.

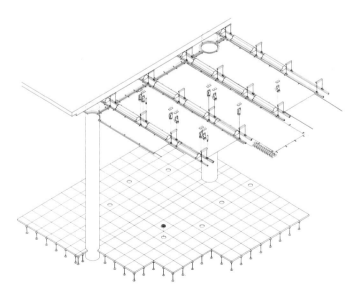

Cutaway axonometric of the ceiling,
lighting, and raised flooring.

Passenger Terminal and Satellites,
Third London Airport

Stansted, England, 1991

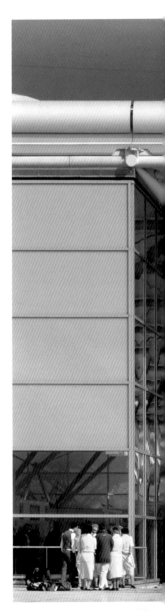

In 1979 the British government authorized the conversion of a former military air base at Stansted into London's third airport. A year later, the British Airports Authority appointed Foster Associates to design the new terminal building, which was to be capable of handling 15 million passengers a year.

When it opened in 1991, the Stansted Terminal signaled a revolution in British airport design. Fifteen percent cheaper than its immediate predecessor, the second terminal at Gatwick (which had been cheaper than the most recent terminal at Heathrow), Stansted was a triumph of engineering, aesthetics, and function. To gauge the magnitude of its achievement it is necessary only to reflect on the way it reintroduced words like "landscaping" and "daylight" into the vocabulary of airport design. The Stansted concept of serviced undercroft and roof umbrella has since become the model for terminal design worldwide.

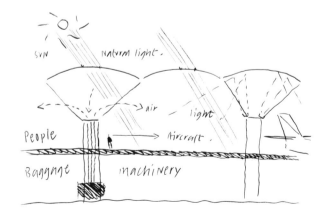

Entrance canopy and Norman Foster sketch, opposite page, of the elements of the Stansted terminal.

Aerial view showing terminal, two satellites, and proposed location of two more.

Nighttime view from parking lot.

Long section showing changes of level.

The open bays of the entrance canopy.

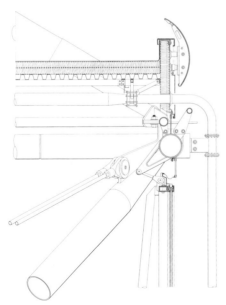

Eaves detail.

The baggage reclaim area.

Daylighting at Stansted depends upon the roof design, a series of parasol structures supported by structural 'trees' that grow from shallow pad foundations below ground level. There are thirty-six of these quadruple tubular steel trees at 36-meter centers, all connected at half their height (apparent ground level) to the coffered concrete concourse floor slab. Twelve meters above their foundations, four tubular steel struts branch out from each tree to support the square grid of 18-meter beams that carries the PVC-covered vaulted metal roof decking that rises a further 3 meters to the top of the vault. The quadruple form of the supporting trees reflects their structural function and their role as service risers through which cabling, air conditioning, smoke extractors, and other services reach the concourse.

Historically, the design of Stansted's structural trees falls somewhere between the 1977 completion of the Sainsbury Centre for Visual Arts and the 1982 completion of the Renault Distribution Centre. Like the Renault building, Stansted is a 'big shed.' But where Renault's PVC roof was penetrated by steel columns and tension rods, Stansted's 50,000-square-meter PVC roof membrane is continuous, with no penetrations, no roof-mounted plant, and no satellite dishes. (They have been

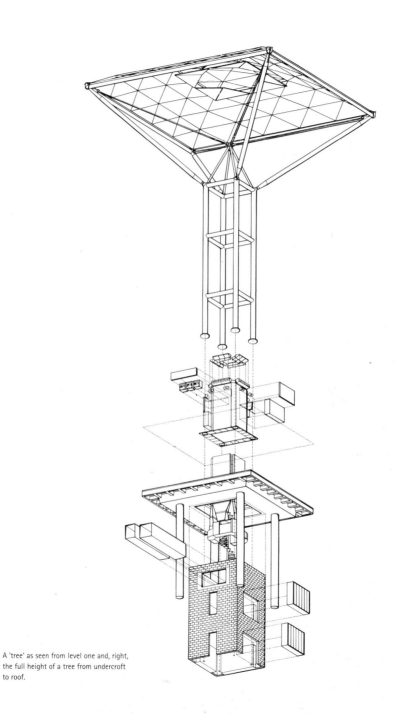

A 'tree' as seen from level one and, right,
the full height of a tree from undercroft
to roof.

Detail of light reflectors in roof vault.

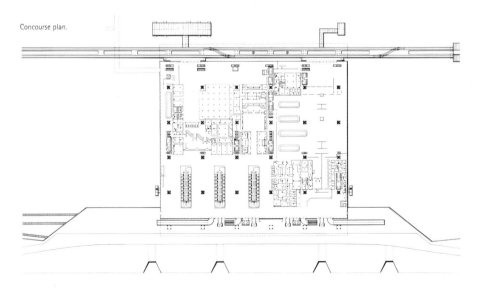

Concourse plan.

banished to the undercroft or to a nearby 'aerial farm'.) This leaves a roof that is unprecedentedly clean as well as apparently weightless: shorn of all auxiliary and servicing functions it delivers a quality of light and space as awe-inspiring as the nave of a Gothic cathedral.

By extensive earth movement the terminal building was made to appear to be on a single level; its buried undercroft of mechanized services enables it to float in the reshaped landscape that surrounds it. For passengers, who will never see beneath its gray granite floor into the immense 'engine room', it will always appear as a single-story building with glass walls and a luminescent roof. Its heavy equipment and railway station are buried below the 'waterline' of the passenger concourse so that the canopy of roof shells can be held aloft like an enormous sail.

It is only after a passenger reaches the shuttle train to the first of what will eventually be four satellite departure lounges that the simplicity of the single level is lost and vertical movement begins. Perhaps it is best to think of the long, thin, vertically stratified satellites as the price that had to be paid for the classic simplicity of the terminal itself, which comes to resemble a capital ship, riding an earth berm 'bow-wave' that hides its 2,500-place parking lot and casts its satellites into the role of escort vessels, cruising on their own landscape 'waves' alongside the hump-backed shuttle maintenance shed.

Principal consultants: Ove Arup & Partners, structural engineers; British Airports Authority, service engineers and cost consultants; Claude Engle, lighting

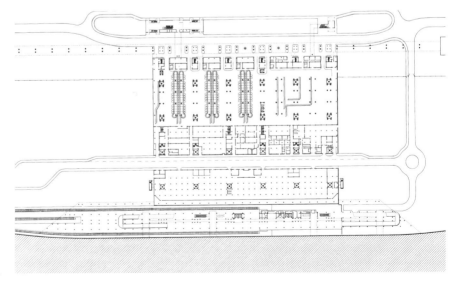

Undercroft plan.

Hong Kong International Airport
Passenger Terminal
Hong Kong, China, 1998

This airport, a successor to the tortuously approached Kai Tak Airport that served Hong Kong until 1998, is the largest in the world, but only if one includes the cost of its massively engineered approach route can it be considered expensive. It is located on a 6-by-3.5-kilometer manmade island off the northern coast of Lantau Island, some 32 kilometers west of the city center.

Great slices have been cut out of the stepping stone islands of Lantau, Ma Wan, and Tsing Yi to make room for a road and rail link that makes it possible to travel from the center of Hong Kong to the airport terminal in thirty minutes. The journey encompasses the massive infrastructural works that make up the rest of the airport project, including a new harbor tunnel and the world's longest double-deck road and rail suspension bridge at Tsing Ma, which carries a six-lane expressway, a mass-transit rail line, and enclosed emergency roads on either side for use in typhoons.

Together with the mast-stayed Kap Shui Mun Bridge that connects Lantau and Ma Wan and sundry viaducts and roadcuts, these feats of civil engineering serve as an appropriate introduction to the airport's grand scale. The complex includes the Ground Transportation Centre, Air Cargo Building, and

Wire frame diagram of roof.

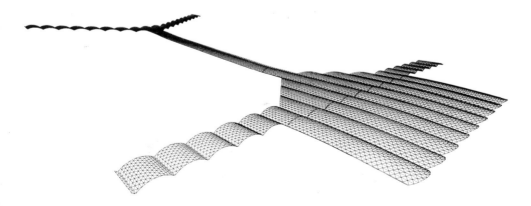

Aerial view.

Long elevation.

Elevational section through east hall.

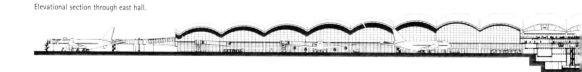

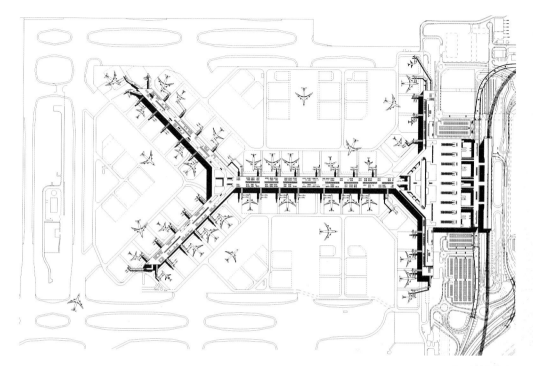

Departures level plan.

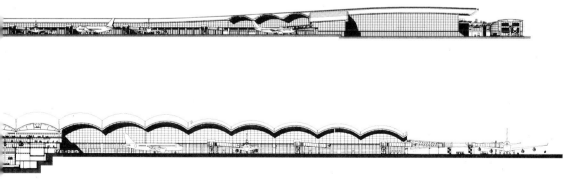

View down spine of terminal concourse
and, below, section through typical roof
vault showing access walkway.

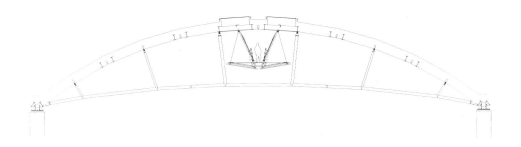

the 1.2-kilometer-long, 520,000-square-meter Passenger Terminal—the largest enclosed public space ever built.

The basement-level rail shuttle and baggage processing areas serving the thirty-eight gates of the distinctive Y-shaped terminal are hidden from view by moving walkways that pass through 30,000 square meters of retail and entertainment space, accommodating some 140 shops and restaurants. Although it opened in the summer of 1998, the terminal building is so vast that parts of it had been completed a year earlier. In addition to the concrete substructure and structural columns, early completions included much of the 45-acre steel diagonal grid roof. The airport's most prominent architectural element, the continuous roof, seen from the air, takes on the shape of a giant bird or a manta ray, wrapped in 4.5 kilometers of glass.

Departure hall / check-in.

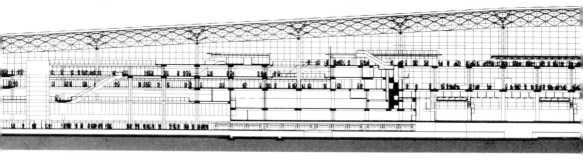

Ground Transportation Centre.

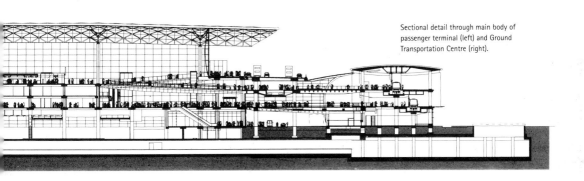

Sectional detail through main body of
passenger terminal (left) and Ground
Transportation Centre (right).

Check-in at dusk and, opposite page,
the view across the departure hall.

Norman Foster: A Global Architecture

The roof was designed in association with structural engineers Ove Arup & Partners and was assembled from 122 site-welded steel lattice shells, each covering nearly 1,300 square meters. Thousands of steel beams were welded together on site on special jigs to produce the huge barrel-vaulted sections, each of which weighs more than 130 tons. These were then lifted by computer-controlled cranes into their final positions. Because the roof slopes longitudinally as well as laterally over its immense run, the bolted joints over the supporting columns were designed to absorb large horizontal and vertical tolerances.

The architects and engineers honed down the kit of parts for the roof to an almost unbelievably small number of standardized components. The triangular ceiling panels that hide the roof decking from the public's gaze are a case in point. There are thousands of these panels, all of them the same size. They not only fit flush between the structural members, but in other locations are suspended as daylight and luminaire reflectors, throwing light back up onto the underside of the roof to create a floating effect that is redoubled by the long vistas within the terminal.

Principal consultants: Mott Consortium, comprised of Mott Connell Ltd., structural engineers; British Airports Authority, airport systems. Other consultants included W.T. & Partners, cost consultants; Fisher Marantz, lighting consultants; Ove Arup & Partners, structural design of terminal roof

Duisburg Energy-Efficient Buildings

Duisburg, Germany:
Business Promotion Center, 1993;
Telematic Center, 1993;
Microelectronic Center, 1996

The three energy-efficient buildings Foster and Partners designed for a business park in Duisburg, Germany, constitute one of the most radical experiments in "environmentally responsible" architecture in Europe. Commissioned in 1988 in association with the German environmental engineering firm Kaiser Bautechnik, the firm created a master plan for the new business park in addition to designing the three buildings.

The first building, completed in spring 1993, was the lens-shaped Business Promotion Center. The 4,000-square-meter, seven-story structure is clad entirely with a double-glass facade system that features controllable sun blinds and operable inner windows. Photovoltaic cells on the downward-curving roof convert the sun's energy into electric power, while solar collectors heat water that is then piped to an absorption cooler. That water is then distributed through radiant panels beneath the concrete floor slabs. The building is so heavily insulated that energy is required

Opposite page: the Business Promotion Center. Below: plan of the Duisburg site.

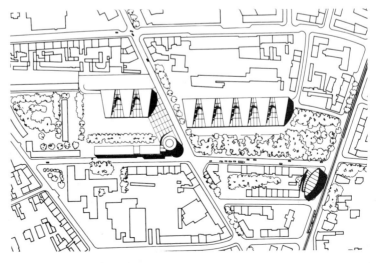

The Business Promotion Center
showing curved double glass facade.

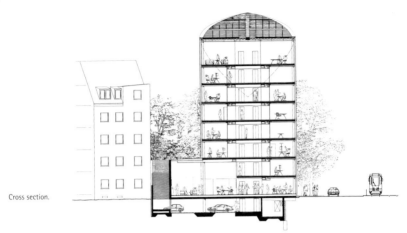

Cross section.

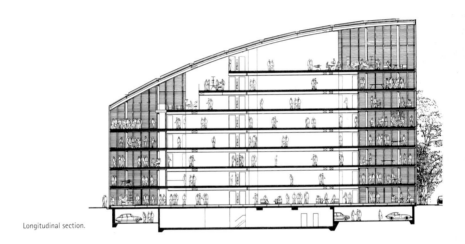

Longitudinal section.

Typical office floor
plan showing narrow
eliptical core.

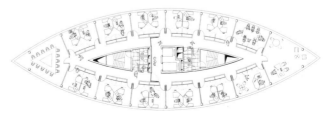

Boardroom interior and terraced offices.

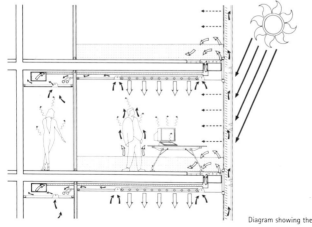

Diagram showing thermal processes.

Exterior view.

only for lighting and cooling. It also shows a profit on energy sold to tenants, subsidizing its operating costs.

The second building completed at Duisburg was the 3,500-square-meter Telematic Center. Cylindrical in form and clad in glass with a double facade like its predecessor, this building features offices arranged around a 11-meter-diameter full-height atrium. The offices house the management of the business park as well as providing space for small- and medium-sized companies. The central ground floor space at the base of the atrium accommodates exhibitions, conferences, seminars, musical and theatrical performances, and a restaurant.

The final Duisburg building is the most ambitious, a $50 million, 15,000-square-meter microelectronics center adjoining a new public park. Taking the form of a long half-barrel-vaulted roof consisting of alternating skylights and

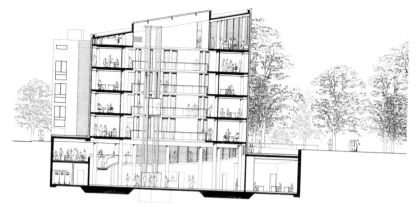

Cross section.

Typical floor plan.

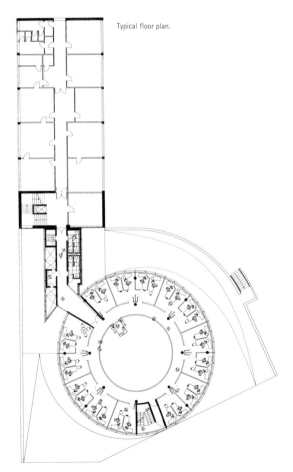

Opposite page: view up into the atrium of the Telematic Center.

Following page: interior of the Microelectronic Center.

Exterior of the Microelectronic Center.

Below: site plan.

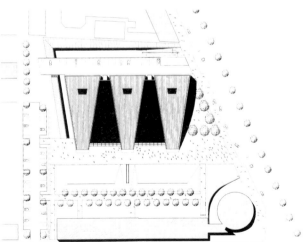

Norman Foster: A Global Architecture

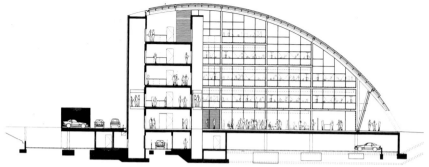

Section through offices.

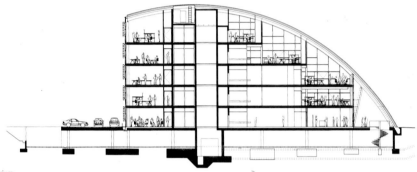

Section through atrium.

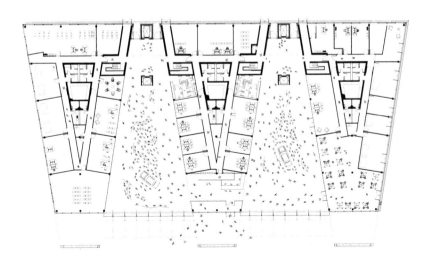

Ground floor plan.

Opposite page: Exterior view of the Microelectronic Center.

Aerial view of the model showing relationship of all three buildings.

opaque panels, the building's 5,000-square-meter first phase contains laboratories, production areas, classrooms, and meeting areas. Subsequent phases will allow business expansion. Within the large climate-controlled envelope of the double-facade building are sheltered buffer zones for exhibitions and service facilities. Energy efficiency is a high priority; the design combines external shading devices with translucent insulation and natural ventilation for all offices that face the park. Initially, the heating and cooling system was to have been fueled by rapeseed oil, a renewable energy source that requires very little processing from crop to fuel. But because that technology was still under development, it was replaced by a connection to the city's coal-fired heating network.

Principal consultants: Ingenieure Büro Dr. Meyer, structural engineers; Kaiser Bautechnik, environmental and energy consultants; Ebert Ingenieure, mechanical and electical engineering; Emmer Pfenninger Partner Ag, cladding consultants; Hohler & Partner, site supervision

Telecommunications Facilities
Barcelona and Santiago de Compostela, Spain, 1992 and 1996

The Barcelona Telecommunications Tower, completed in 1992, was a breakthrough in the design of microwave antennae, combining the functions of many existing masts into a single elegant structure. Foster and Partners' competition-winning design is a 288-meter, cable-stayed tower only 4.5 meters in diameter, tapering to a 0.3-meter-diameter radio mast at its top.

Near the midpoint of the mast is a thirteen-story, trochoidal-shaped structure that supports dishes and antennae, surrounded by a perimeter structure of stainless-steel grillwork. This structure is suspended from the central tower by three primary trusses and tethered to the mountainside by pre-tensioned steel cables. Located on the summit of one of the Tibidabo Mountains overlooking the city, the mast was completed in time for the 1992 Barcelona Olympics. It has since become a symbol of the city.

As in Barcelona, the accumulation of telecommunications masts on Monte Pedroso ridge overlooking Santiago de Compostela was disturbing civic authorities. In 1994 Foster and Partners was invited to propose a solution. Foster's suggestion was not a single tall mast, since there was no need to rise more than

Partial world ranking of telecommunications towers compared to the Sagrada Familia cathedral.

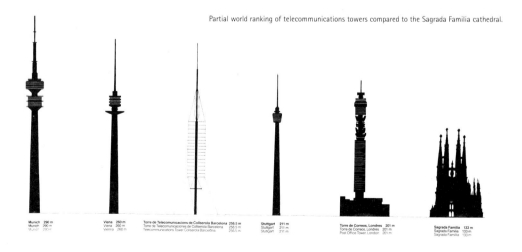

Munich 290 m	Viena 260 m	Torre de Telecomunicacions de Collserola Barcelona 256.5 m	Stuttgart 211 m	Torre de Correos, Londres 201 m	Sagrada Familia 133 m
Munich 290 m	Viena 260 m	Torre de Telecomunicaciones de Collserola Barcelona 256.5 m	Stuttgart 211 m	Torre de Correos, Londres 201 m	Sagrada Familia 133 m
Munich 290 m	Vienna 260 m	Telecommunications Tower Collserola Barcelona 256.5 m	Stuttgart 211 m	Post Office Tower, London 201 m	Sagrada Familia 133 m

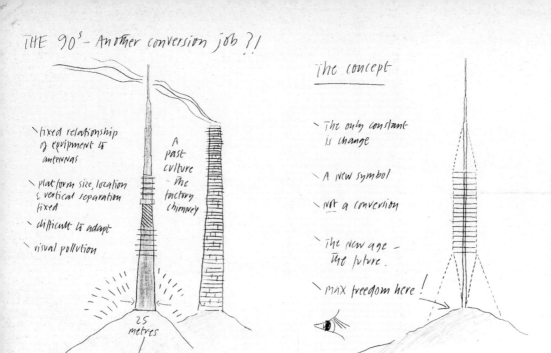

THE 90's - Another conversion job?!

- fixed relationship of equipment & antennas
- platform size, location & vertical separation fixed
- difficult to adapt
- visual pollution

A past culture - The factory chimney

25 metres

The concept

- The only constant is change
- A new symbol
- not a conversion
- The new age - The future.
- max freedom here!

Norman Foster

Concept sketches by Norman Foster.

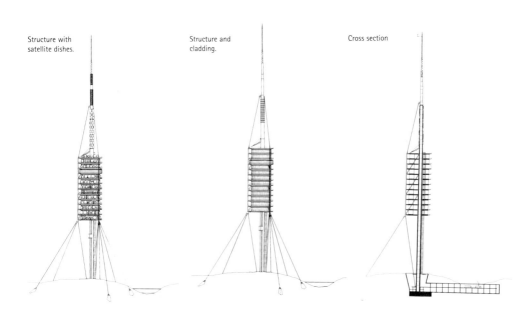

Structure with satellite dishes.

Structure and cladding.

Cross section

Exterior view at night.

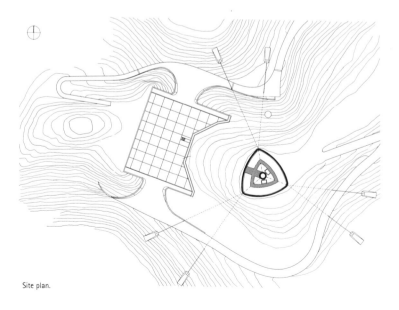

Site plan.

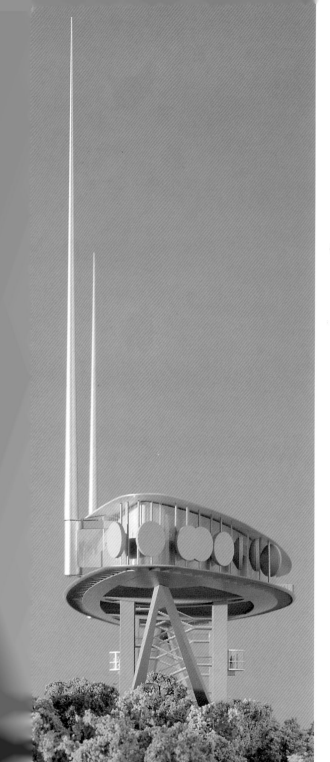

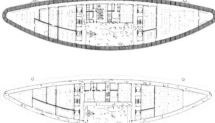

Model view of the Santiago de Compostela Telecommunications Tower.

Main level and mezzanine level plans.

Cross section

25 meters above the wooded ridge, but rather a 1,400-square-meter steel and aluminum platform that could satisfy the needs of all its telecommunications users.

Elliptical in plan, the proposed Santiago Telecommunications Facility is intended to provide separate facilities for each transmission user, with direct access to transmission equipment and masts provided by a perimeter walkway. Part of the platform is to be open to the public as a viewing gallery with a spectacular panorama of the city and the surrounding countryside. Access to the platform is provided by transparent elevators attached to the legs of the reinforced-concrete platform's support structure.

Principal consultants: Ove Arup & Partners, CAST, structural engineers; Davis Langdon & Everest, cost consultants; MC-2, specialist engineers; BMT Fluid Mechanics Ltd. and Oxford University Wind Tunnel, wind engineering

East elevation.

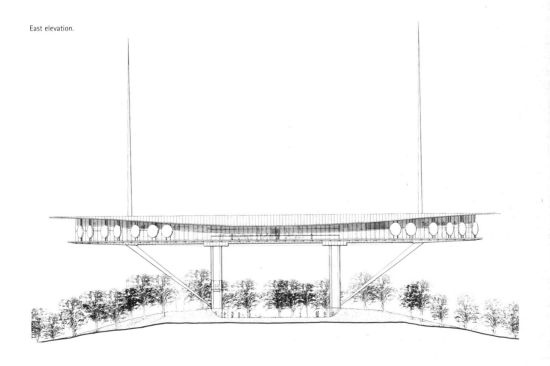

Millennium Tower Projects

Tokyo, Japan, and London, England, 1989–97

Developed for the Obayashi Corporation of Tokyo, Foster's first super-tall skyscraper project was commissioned in 1989. After going through several stages of development, it emerged as an attenuated helical steel needle that would rise 840 meters from a site a mile offshore in Tokyo Bay, where it would be piled into the seabed.

Almost twice the height of the world's tallest buildings, the twin Petronas Towers in Kuala Lumpur, Malaysia, the Tokyo Millennium Tower was planned as a 1.04-million-square-meter commercial development on 170 circular decks of diminishing diameter, emerging from a marina at its base and constituting a serviced floor area sufficient for a small town of some 50,000 people. Inside the glass-clad envelope, facilities would have consisted not only of offices and hotels but also shops, entertainment areas, and apartments. Passengers and goods would be transported within the needle by means of three interconnected systems: a funicular railway stopping at sky lobbies located at every thirtieth floor, with cars capable of carrying up to 160 persons; conventional banks of express elevators serving the floors between sky lobbies; and escalators and stairs serving adjacent floors within specific multistory zones.

While work on the design continued for some time, the project eventually fell victim to the decline of the Japanese real estate market in the early 1990s and was put on indefinite hold. However, the design work overlapped with the construction of the Commerzbank in Frankfurt and then found further relevance with another super-tall scheme, the $640 million London Millennium Tower, a project that originated with the Trafalgar House real estate company and was taken over by its successor, the Norwegian Kvaerner engineering group.

The London Millennium Tower was designed for a site at the heart of the city that had been cleared after a terrorist bomb exploded in 1993. The glass, steel, and concrete structure was intended to rise 385 meters above the city's medieval street pattern. The tower's proportions somewhat resembled those of a wide-bodied jet. Within its glass envelope, the tower would have offered 160,000 square meters of unobstructed office space stacked in 2,000-square-meter floor plates in the lower portion of the tower. Long-span structures would have done away with a central core and mid-span columns.

A sunset view of the Tokyo Millennium Tower.

The marina around the base of the building.

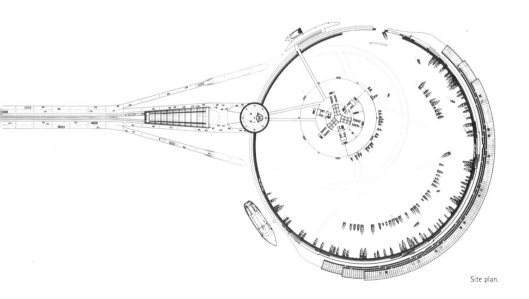

Site plan.

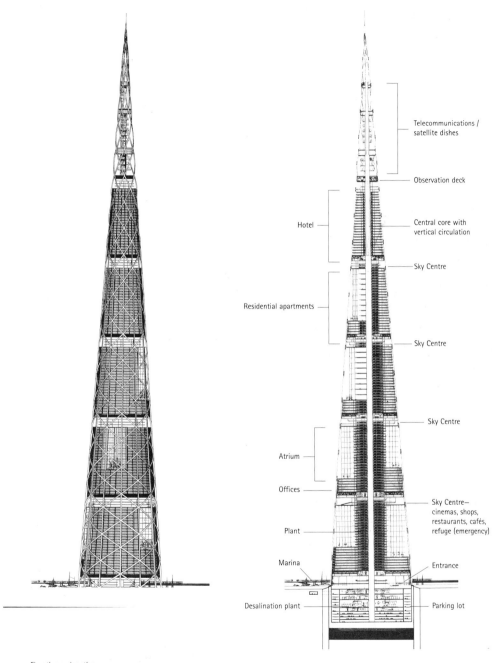

Telecommunications /
satellite dishes

Observation deck

Hotel

Central core with
vertical circulation

Sky Centre

Residential apartments

Sky Centre

Sky Centre

Atrium

Offices

Sky Centre—
cinemas, shops,
restaurants, cafés,
refuge (emergency)

Plant

Marina

Entrance

Desalination plant

Parking lot

Elevation and section.

In addition there would have been 4,000 square meters of retail space in the podium, more than seventy luxury apartments at the top of the tower, and a public observation deck above that, with a 360-degree view of London and beyond. As with the Tokyo Millennium Tower, vertical transportation within would have been advanced, incorporating express elevators that parked out of their shafts, sky lobbies, and escalators. The tower was planned as a mixed-use project, combining shopping, entertainment, commercial, and residential facilities—an energy-efficient, vertical town alive twenty-four hours a day.

Reactions to the London Millennium Tower were mixed from the outset. Unveiled in fall 1996, it remained contentious for a year before the developers wearied of the struggle and developed an alternative strategy with Foster and Partners. While even its most hostile critics never disputed that the tower was economically viable or technically feasible, the official consensus remained against it.

Tokyo Millennium Tower
Principal consultant: Obayashi Corporation
London Millennium Tower
Principal consultants: Ove Arup & Partners, structural engineers; J. Roger Preston & Partners, service engineers; Jones Lang Wootton and BH2, real estate consultants

Commerzbank Headquarters
Frankfurt, Germany, 1997

There is no country in Europe more dedicated to the Green agenda than Germany, particularly in matters relating to building. For this reason alone it seemed likely that Foster Associates' victory in the 1991 international competition to design a headquarters building for Commerzbank would mark a decisive step forward in its development of a more environmentally responsive architecture. The result has not been disappointing.

Interior view showing four-story 'sky gardens.'

The fifty-three-story Commerzbank began where the Hongkong and Shanghai Bank ended. The double-height terraces of the earlier building were originally conceived as gardens in the sky but were never landscaped. In Frankfurt the idea returned, but this time as part of a 300-meter tower—the tallest occupied building in Europe and nearly twice as tall as the Hong Kong bank. And the sky gardens are now associated with a natural ventilation system using a double facade made possible by technology inconceivable in 1978.

The Commerzbank's 100,000 square meters of floor space is stacked on a surprisingly small footprint in the heart of Frankfurt's banking district. The building is triangular in plan, with three 'petals' of office floors arranged around a 'stem' in the form of a giant atrium, which provides stack-effect ventilation in stages up the building. There is no central core; elevators, stairs, services, and other facilities are located in the three corners of the tower. Pairs of vertical structural masts

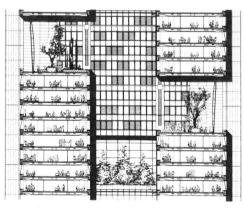

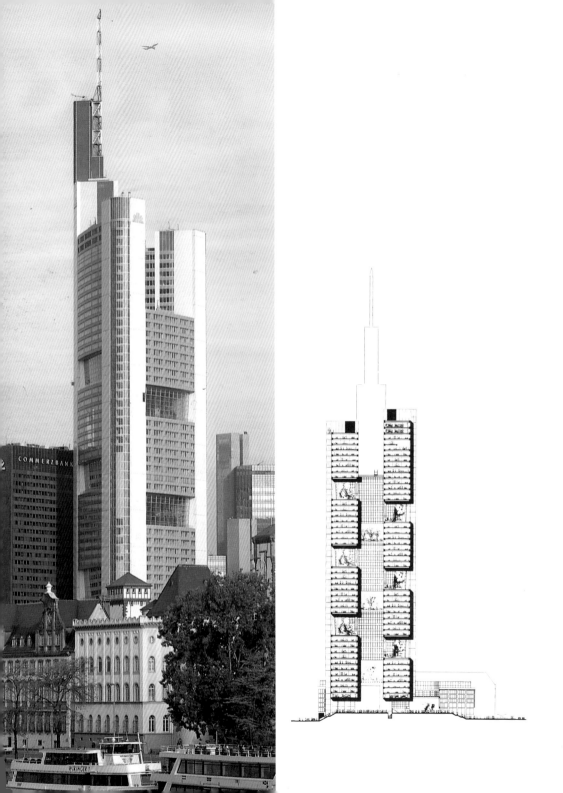

Left to right: Proximity to river. Section through tower showing sky gardens. System of natural ventilation using stack effect. Combined internal and external views from a typical office.

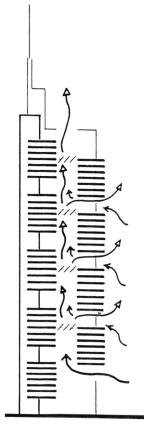

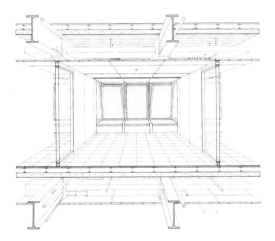

Left: sectional perspective of long-span office floor construction.

Top and opposite page: view looking up the central atrium.

built into these corner structures are linked by eight-story Vierendeel girders, which in turn carry the clear-spanning office floors from corner to corner. All offices can be naturally ventilated by means of operable windows in the inner facade skin. The outer skin remains closed; only a controlled volume of air comes through dedicated intakes. Four-story-high gardens alternate with the eight floors of offices, stepping around the facets of the triangular tower as it rises and ensuring that every inward-facing office enjoys a garden view as well as a long-distance view over the city.

At ground level the tower stands alongside the existing Commerzbank headquarters. Remodeling the adjacent buildings and inserting a grand *escalier* entrance to the tower has created a new public open space, a winter garden with restaurants, cafés, and a space for performances and exhibitions.

Principal consultants: Ove Arup & Partners with Krebs & Kiefer, structural engineers; J. Roger Preston & Partners with Pettersen & Ahrends, service engineers; Davis Langdon & Everest, cost consultants; The Quickborner Team, space planners

Ground floor plan.

View showing the building in downtown Frankfurt.

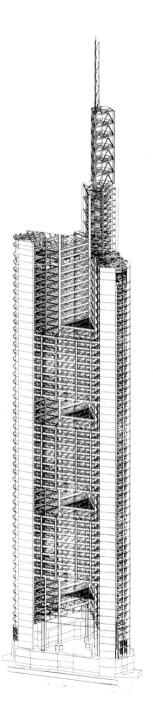

Cutaway structural isometric.

Sackler Galleries, Royal Academy of Arts
London, England, 1991

American Air Museum, Imperial War Museum
Duxford, England, 1997

Today, the Sackler Galleries at the Royal Academy in London are rec-ognized as a turning point in the relationship between the old and the new in architecture. When Norman Foster was commissioned to refurbish three decrepit Victorian galleries in 1985, however, he was not an obvious choice for the task. Although he had dealt with con-servation issues before, he had never worked on a historic building.

Some of the architect's fresh approach to the Royal Academy project may have come from this lack of conventional experience. But part also came from years of work with adventurous commercial clients and a legendary attention to quality and detail. Never content merely to follow a client's brief, however small the job, Foster's office invariably makes a deep study of its client's organization.

At the Royal Academy, the Foster team-members soon saw that there would be little benefit in improving the old Diploma Galleries without improving the means of access to them, so they began to look for a better line of approach. They found it in the junction between the original Burlington House—the creation of several architects including Colen Campbell, William Kent, and Samuel Ware—and the main gallery extension added by Sidney Smirke in 1867. Their key discovery was a 4.2-meter slot between the two buildings they called 'the gap,' crossed by the academy's main stair-case and partially blocked by ancillary facilities. Embarking on an 'archaeological voyage of discovery,' the Foster team explored these gloomy, forgotten spaces and began to think of reclaiming the gap for a new staircase to the Diploma Galleries.

Opening up the gap exposed the garden facade of Burlington

The restored Burlington House garden facade inside 'the gap', right, and, opposite page, the glass-enclosed elevator.

House, not seen for more than a hundred years, as well as the south wall of Smirke's gallery extension. Foster wanted to restore both of these facades, then insert a freestanding structure inside the gap that would not only include a new staircase to the Diploma Galleries, but also expand at the top into a new sculpture gallery. The project, including the almost complete reconstruction of the Diploma Galleries, was enthusiastically endorsed by the American philanthropist Arthur Sackler, whose patronage enabled the work to proceed with an enhanced budget.

The gap was re-opened and its two facades restored to form the sides of a new access lobby. At the top, the space is closed by the new sculpture gallery's floor, which, as elsewhere, was edged in glass to emphasize its separateness. The roof and north wall of the gallery were enclosed with white laminated glass, supported by outrigged steel portal frames barely visible from inside. Access to the rebuilt galleries, renamed the Sackler Galleries, is by a new steel and glass staircase and glass elevator in the gap itself. The picture galleries were completely

Long section looking toward
Burlington House elevation.

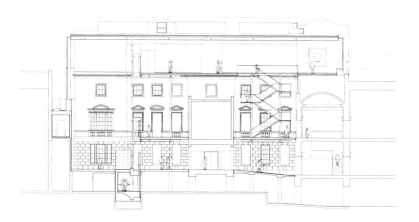

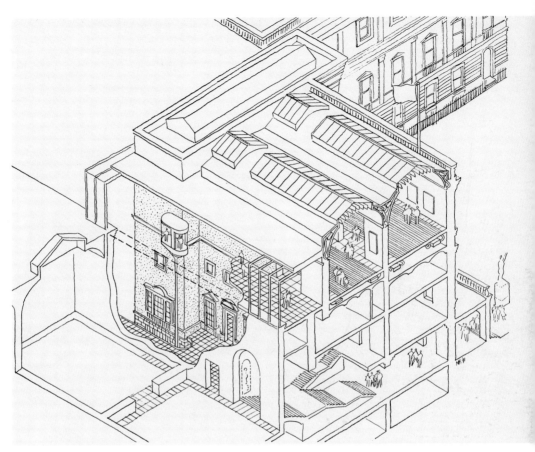

Cutaway axonometric sketch.

Ground floor plan.

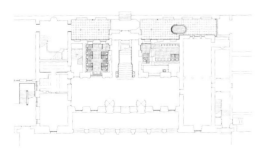

Second floor plan.

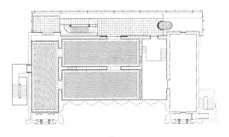

Interior, opposite page, showing suspended glass screen wall.

The blister-shaped museum from the airfield, right, by day and, following pages, by night.

rebuilt as air-conditioned, light-controlled, barrel-vaulted, white-painted rooms, their complex services hidden behind ceilings and raised floors.

The minimalism of the modern parts of this project—its glass roof, glass and steel staircase, noiseless elevator—throws its historical components into dramatic prominence. A visitor to the sculpture gallery stands on a level with the cornice of the Smirke building, in effect in the air, in a place that did not previously exist. The modest 340 square meters of floor space recovered and created at the Royal Academy has a directness and honesty that is evident to every visitor. The relationship of old and new does not require explanation, nor is there any question that the effect achieved was intentional.

The magazine *Modern Painters* asked Sir Norman Foster if, given an unlimited budget, he would not have preferred to design something that would have made the gap entirely his own. "It is entirely my own," he replied. "It is a deliberate interpretation of how you relate the old to the new and get something richer and more dynamic out of both."

Some seven years after Her Majesty the Queen opened the Sackler Galleries, a very different kind of Foster-designed gallery opened at the Imperial War Museum at Duxford in Cambridgeshire. The $16 million, 7,400-square-meter American Air Museum houses the Imperial War Museum's collection of thirty-eight U.S. combat aircraft, the largest such collection outside the United States. Duxford itself is a former air base and served from 1943 to 1945 as headquarters of the U.S. Air Force's 78th fighter group.

Interior view showing toplit mezzanine.

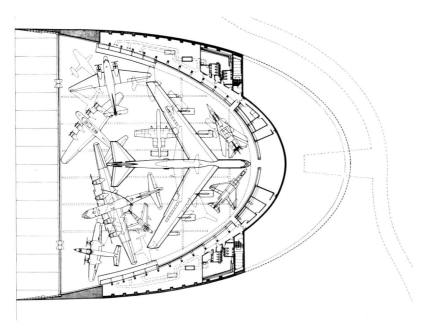

Ground floor plan.

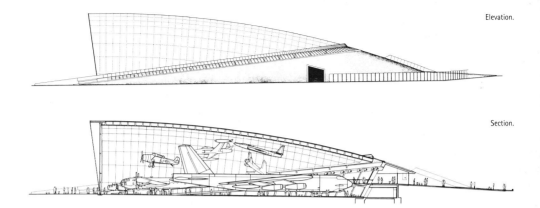

Elevation.

Section.

Although the museum opened in 1997, its design dates from almost the same period as that of the Sackler Galleries. Problems financing the project delayed its construction for nearly ten years, and were resolved only through fund-raising efforts in the United States, over 500,000 of whose servicemen were based in England during World War II.

The museum is a partly buried, blister-shaped structure of distinctly aeronautical appearance, except for its full-height glass front wall. Partly elliptical in plan, it features a single large exhibition space, with support facilities in the rear. Aircraft are parked on the floor of the museum and suspended from its concrete roof in attitudes of flight. The largest aircraft, a Boeing B-52 bomber that is 16 meters high and has a 60-meter wingspan, largely determined the size of the museum, which is up to 100 meters wide and 91 meters deep. The complex geometry of the streamlined roof, which employs long-spanning concrete arches at its widest point adjacent to the glass wall and takes the form of a shallow dome at the rear, enabled the entire structure to be cast on site in only five segments. The concrete roof's interior presents an undecorated finish, enhancing the design's no-frills, military feeling.

Sackler Galleries
Principal consultants: YRM Anthony Hunt Associates, structural engineers; Julian Harrap Architects, conservation architects; Davis Langdon & Everest, cost consultants
American Air Museum
Principal consultants: Ove Arup & Partners, structural engineers; J. Roger Preston & Partners and Aerospace Structural and Mechanical Engineering, service engineers

Exterior view at night.

Faculty of Law, University of Cambridge
Cambridge, England, 1995

The University of Cambridge's Faculty of Law is located on a site already populated by significant modern buildings by Sir Hugh Casson and Neville Conder, Sir James Stirling, and Leslie Martin. Its rectangular plan is cut off at a sharp diagonal angle that corresponds to the angle of the nearby Faculty of History by Sir James Stirling and preserves existing circulation routes. Above ground, the glass-clad building is a four-story, propped cantilever structure; below ground is a partial double-height basement that accommodates raked lecture rooms.

Encompassing some 9,000 square meters, the whole structure is inserted into a glazed, tubular steel, triangulated structural envelope that is curved to a barrel-vaulted section spanning 35 meters.

Early concept sketch by Norman Foster.

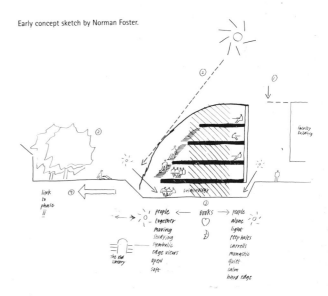

Entrance canopy roof detail.

Ground floor plan.

Second floor plan.

Third floor plan.

View of the model.

Cross section.

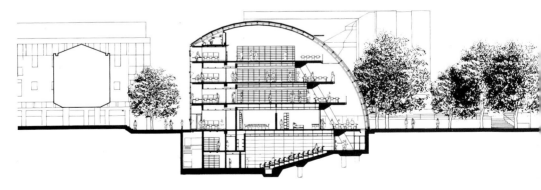

Two interior views showing, opposite page, the junction of the curved glass envelope and, above, the cantilevered balconies.

This distance includes a section of the envelope that is finished in stainless steel and projects outward to shade the upper floors. It terminates in a south-facing wall clad in reconstituted Portland stone and white glass with clear opening lights.

Three above-ground floors house the Squire Law Library, the principal occupant of the building. The rest of the building accommodates five new auditoriums, seminar rooms, common rooms, bookstores, and administrative offices. The triangulated glass envelope facing north is designed to have a very high thermal performance and to admit the maximum amount of daylight. A full-height atrium brings daylight to the heart of the building; natural ventilation is used throughout, except in the basement lecture rooms, which are air-conditioned.

Principal consultants: Anthony Hunt Associates, structural engineers; YRM Engineers, service engineers; Davis Langdon & Everest, cost consultants; Sandy Brown Associates, acoustic architects

Scottish Exhibition and Conference Centre
Glasgow, Scotland, 1997

Sir Norman Foster began his career with inexpensive industrial buildings on provincial trading estates; he earned the position he now enjoys by applying the same methods to larger commissions on more prestigious sites. But Foster never lost the capacity to return to the economical mode of his early years. He still harbors an affection for standard-profile metal cladding, and he and his staff invariably find ways and places to use it that other architects would never consider.

The Industrial Theatre and Exhibition Hall at the Scottish Exhibition and Conference Centre in Glasgow, popularly known as the 'Armadillo,' is a good example of this. Here a precast and bonded concrete block auditorium anchors a series of curved tubular steel trusses, over which are 'flopped' great parallelograms of profiled aluminum. This material arrived on site in giant rolls. Once in place, it follows a curved profile equivalent to that of the surface of a cylinder 38 meters in diameter. The ingenuity of this arrangement, which required no complicated rebending of the standardized industrial cladding, made genuine savings possible without the loss of architectural drama. This, of course, is

Below: CAD perspective of the roof structure.

Opposite page: Detail of the roof from below.

Following pages: exterior view of main entrance.

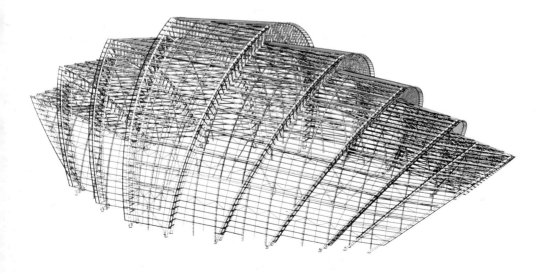

Hotel, Conference Centre, and dock
crane seen across former shipping basin.

Longitudinal section.

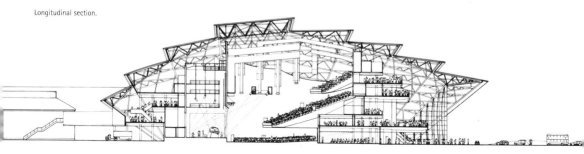

Norman Foster: A Global Architecture

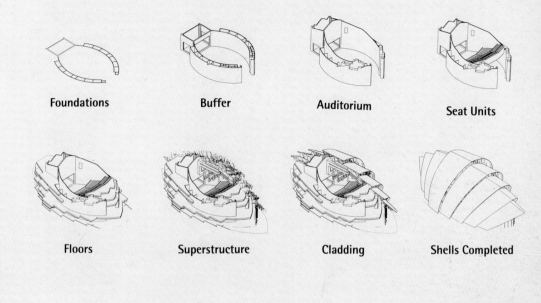

Foundations **Buffer** **Auditorium** **Seat Units**

Floors **Superstructure** **Cladding** **Shells Completed**

Construction sequence.

Cross sections.

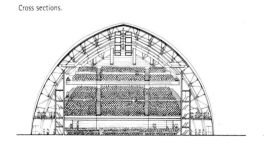

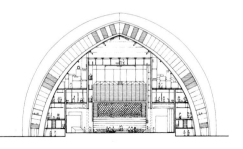

Ground floor plan.

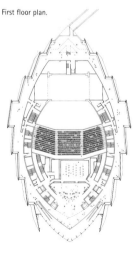

First floor plan.

Second floor plan.

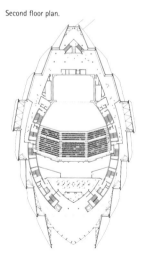

Opposite page: interior view of
auditorium.

expected of Foster and Partners. But there is more to it than that. It stands as proof that Foster's skills with limited resources have not given way to new ones, but instead have been stored for more than thirty years, ready to be used whenever occasion serves.

In its economy, the Armadillo is almost an industrial building. The only truly expensive piece in it is the tall glass screen that rises above the east-facing entrance. Everything else, from the painted concrete to the large areas of medium-density fiberboard, is cheap: cheaper than most industrial buildings, almost as cheap as military or prison architecture. The construction cost was under $42 million for 1,300 square meters of highly serviced and partially air-conditioned conference and exhibition space—and a facility finished ahead of time and already booked five years in advance.

Given this list of plusses, there can hardly be any argument against the clever use of common industrial materials to clad such a high-profile public building. Not every detail of the Armadillo was created especially for it and it alone. It is more like a car designed from the outset to facilitate its manufacture: lighter, cheaper, and quicker.

Principal consultants: Ove Arup & Partners, structural and service engineers; Gardiner & Theobald, cost consultants; Sandy Brown Associates, acoustic and theater design consultants

Third floor plan.

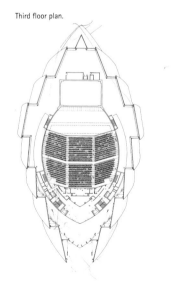

Fourth floor plan.

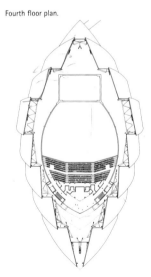

Fifth floor plan.

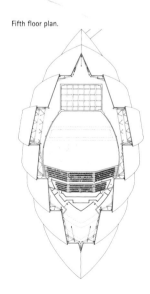

Congress Center
Valencia, Spain, 1998

The Valencia Congress Center is the centerpiece of a new area of urban development in Valencia; its distinctive outline has made it a landmark on the approach to the city from the northwest. The 18,000-square-meter reinforced-concrete, steel, and aluminum conference center is planned in the shape of an eye and defined by two opposing arcs of unequal length. Fanning out from the tighter curve of the western facade, which conceals service areas and the center's more strictly functional elements, are three auditoriums and seminar rooms. The largest auditorium can accommodate 1,463 people; the second, 468; and the smallest, 250.

Unlike most auditorium complexes, which typically exclude natural light, the Congress Center is a transparent enclosure; only the auditoriums themselves are blacked out. Elsewhere, daylight penetrates deep into the heart of the building. Running the length of the eastern edge are the building's open public areas,

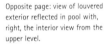

Opposite page: view of louvered exterior reflected in pool with, right, the interior view from the upper level.

Entrance elevation.

Night view of vestibule elevation.

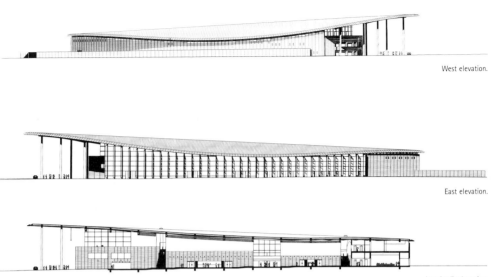

West elevation.

East elevation.

Longitudinal section.

Interior of main auditorium.

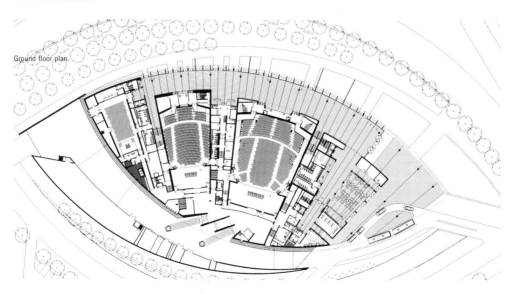

Ground floor plan.

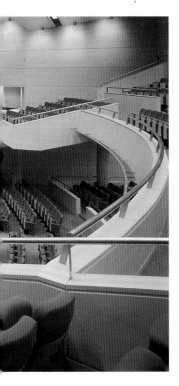

Internal foyer.

including a wide foyer from which the conference facilities are reached. This looks out onto a park with shade trees and seating, reached by a series of footbridges over pools of water that grow larger as they sweep south.

The 9,000-square-meter, two-layer roof's zinc-coated aluminum skin is raised above the main reinforced-concrete roof slab to encourage cooling air currents between the two, optimizing the building's passive thermal performance. Inclined from end to end, the roof floats above the building, rising at the southern end and above the main entrance to its maximum height of approximately 20 meters.

Principal consultants: Ove Arup & Partners, structural engineers; J. Roger Preston & Partners, service engineers; Davis Langdon & Everest, cost consultants; Arup Acoustics, acoustic consultants

Lycée Albert Camus
Fréjus, France, 1993

The Lycée Albert Camus is a successful example of the adjustment of a naturally ventilated modern building to the demands of a particular location, in this case the Mediterranean town of Fréjus on the Côte d'Azur. The school, which can accommodate up to 900 students, offers a mix of academic and vocational instruction for pupils in their last three years of full-time education.

Foster and Partners won the commission in a limited competition held in 1991. There were two key requirements: the design should permit rapid construction, and the building should be able to stand up to heavy use. The architects' design, a 16,000-square-meter, two-story structure, occupies a long rectangle whose central axis is an internal street. Modular facilities that make use of standardized concrete structural frames and roof shells are repeated along the length of this street. Aluminum-framed glazed partitions open onto the outside of the building as well as to the internal street. The concrete roofs give a high thermal mass to the building, while the repetition of modules permitted the use of high-quality metal-faced formwork to produce excellent

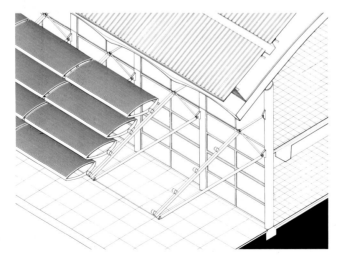

Axonometric detail showing the metal and concrete roofs and the *brise soleil* mounting system.

Shaded outdoor teaching areas.

South side showing concrete roof shells.

Cross section showing double-height "street."

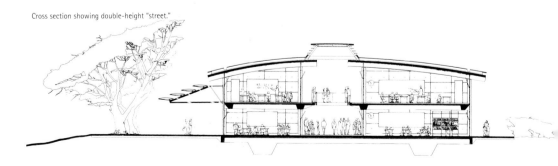

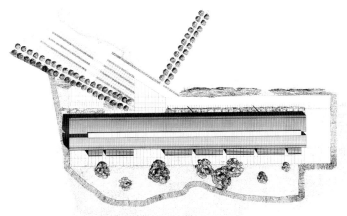

Site plan.

Ground floor plan.

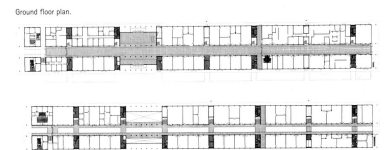

First floor plan.

Opposite page: the double-height internal "street" runs the full length of the building.

concrete finishes at a relatively low cost. The school was completed in just twelve months and within its $15 million budget.

The architects sought to provide a comfortable internal environment throughout the year with the maximum use of passive systems. To this end, the double-height internal street provides a natural stack-effect ventilation space, drawing air through the classrooms, while the roof's metal outer skin, held clear of each concrete shell, ensures air movement between the two and produces a cooling effect. An extensive array of *brises soleil* protects the south side of the building and the clerestory windows above the internal street from overhead sunlight, but permits low-angle winter sun to penetrate the interior.

Principal consultants: Ove Arup & Partners, structural engineers; J. Roger Preston & Partners, service engineers; Davis Langdon Everest, cost consultants

The Great Glass House emerging
from the landscape.

Norman Foster: A Global Architecture

National Botanic Garden of Wales
Llanarthne, Wales, 1998

The centerpiece of the new National Botanic Garden of Wales, on the restored and re-landscaped 560-acre grounds of Middleton Hall, a country estate in South Wales, is a great toroidal glass enclosure, elliptical in plan, measuring 95 meters by 55 meters, rising organically from the landscape. The dome will be completed in 1999; the Botanic Garden is scheduled to open in 2000, in time for the millennial celebrations.

The original Middleton Hall was demolished in the 1950s. The outline of its plan will be traced with hedges, and its stables and double-walled garden restored. All this serves as a setting for the Great Glass House, a single-span steel and glass structure

Plan of the gardens.

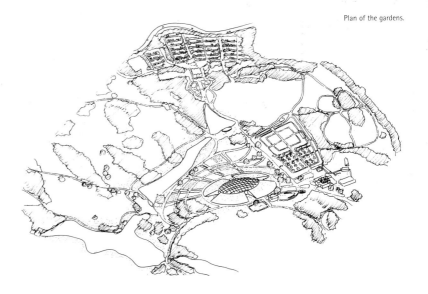

Sectioned model of the Great Glass
House.

Longitudinal section.

Cross section.

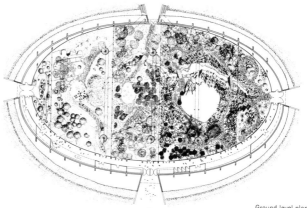

Ground level plan.

supported entirely at its perimeter. The modern structure was designed to maximize light transmission into its 4,000-square-meter interior, a single volume that houses 100,000 plants in a Mediterranean climate. The base plan of the oval is tilted, creating a natural grassed bank to the north to protect the interior from northerly weather, and opening up views of the countryside to the south. There is generous ventilation through the glazed enclosure to encourage healthy growth of plants and avoid overheating in summer.

Principal consultants: Anthony Hunt Associates, structural engineers; Max Fordham and Partners, service engineers; Symonds, cost consultants; Colvin and Moggridge, external landscape architects; Gustafson Porter, internal landscape architects

Interior of the model of the Great Glass House.

Great Court, British Museum
London, England, 2000

The great square court of the British Museum is one of London's lost architectural spaces. Nearly as big as Hanover Square, it was originally intended to be the heart of the museum, which was completed by Sir Robert Smirke in 1847. Just ten years later, though, the court was overwhelmed by Sidney Smirke's epic 42.5-meter-diameter round reading room and its associated book stacks, which effectively sealed off the circulation hub of the building. Remarkably, it is only now, almost a century and a half later, that the space has again become available, following the completion of the new British Library and the removal of its vast collection of books.

Foster and Partners' approach to the reclamation of this space follows the technique of letting old and new coexist that the firm pioneered at the Sackler Galleries in London and in the Reichstag in Berlin. A new stone floor for the court will link all the principal spaces of the museum's main floor, including the round reading room at the court's center, while the space between the reading room and the court's surrounding walls will be roofed using

Wire frame diagram of Great Court roof.

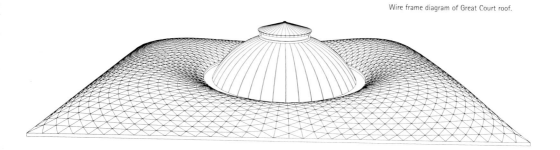

Aerial views showing the British
Museum before and after recovery
of Great Court.

Computer-generated view of the
reopened Great Court.

Amenity accomodation beneath the
new roof of the Great Court.

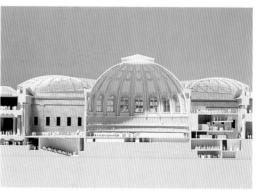

Section showing exploitation of
new levels in the Great Court.

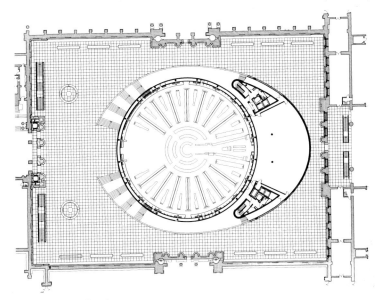

Ground floor plan of the Great Court.

a glazed lightweight steel frame to maximize daylighting. In this way, the Great Court will again become a focal point for the whole museum and will open outside normal museum hours to create a new public space for London.

It will be possible to reach the upper level galleries from the new enclosed Great Court by way of a grand double staircase circling the round reading room as part of a new elliptical structure. Below the court, a new education center will be built with seminar rooms, two auditoriums, and new exhibition spaces for the African collection. The celebrated round reading room will house a new museum library and information center, open to the general public for the first time.

Principal consultants: Buro Happold, structural engineers; Davis Langdon Everest, cost consultants

New German Parliament, Reichstag
Berlin, Germany, 1999

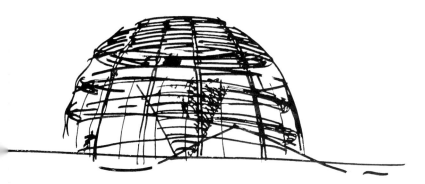

Phoenix-like, the battered Reichstag has risen from the ashes of its checkered history. At a cost of $450 million, the former home of German democracy, gutted by fire at the beginning of the Nazi era, bombed in World War II, and left derelict until the 1960s, when it was partially repaired and used as a conference center, has undergone a radical transformation. In spring 1999, it reopened as the new home of the Bundestag, a state-of-the-art, solar-powered, naturally ventilated parliament for the reunified Germany.

Foster and Partners' original commission, won in a 1992 competition, was for a considerable enlargement to the original building to accommodate a podium for a public forum. Since then, the commission has been scaled back to the area within the walls of the original building, and it has taken on a more symbolic nature. Keeping in mind the building's political history—both the cradle and grave of Germany democracy—the Foster team concentrated on making the processes of the German parliament more transparent. They also wanted to turn the building into a living museum of its own history, including preserving graffiti left behind by the Red Army in 1945; increase public access; and install advanced, low-energy systems appropriate to the twenty-first century.

The building's main entrance has been reopened and the principal

raised level has been restored, along with the original courtyards and the original number of floors. The roof has been transformed into a public area with a restaurant and terraces as well as a kind of observation deck for the parliamentary process in the plenary chamber below. The most prominent new structure is a glass cupola over this debating chamber, which replaces the original copper and glass dome destroyed after the war. The new cupola not only serves ventilation functions but also encloses a huge 'daylight chandelier,' an inverted cone fitted with photovoltaic cells and hundreds of mirrors that direct daylight down into the chamber while reflecting views of the sky for those below. Spiral ramps inside the cupola provide access to a high-level viewing platform.

Sensitivity to history, natural ventilation, non-polluting power sources, and the extensive use of daylighting characterize the new Bundestag. The last of these depends heavily upon the use of high-performance glass, the prominence of which will be the most obvious external sign of the reconstruction.

Internally, one of the most significant changes is almost invisible. "We asked the [competition] jury if they knew how much it cost to run the Reichstag as it was," Foster recalled. "But none of them knew. So we told them and showed them how we could do it for a fraction of that sum. That way the savings would eventually pay back the cost of part of the work."

Longitudinal section.

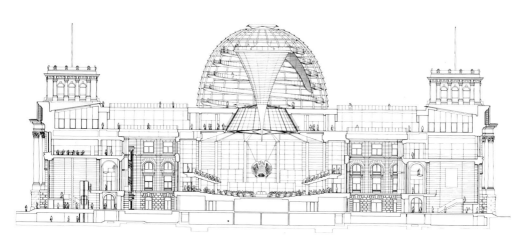

The west lobby looking into the chamber.

Following pages: the public on the roof of parliament: thousands of visitors every day ascend the spiralling ramps to visit the public viewing platform.

Cross section.

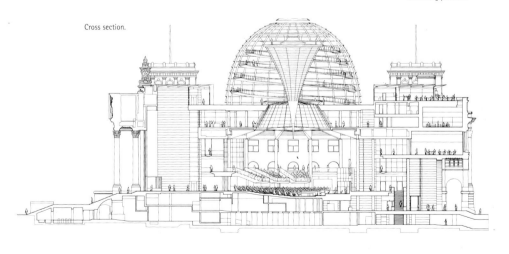

New German Parliament, Reichstag

Ground floor plan.

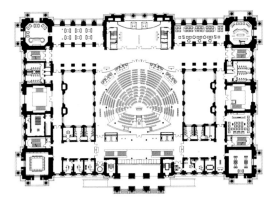

Roof level plan.

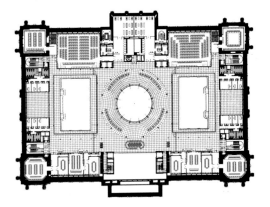

Opposite page: interior view of the chamber

In time, this promise has been kept. The new heating and cooling system is powered by vegetable oil made from rapeseed, an economical fuel that requires little processing. And sophisticated new heat-recovery and energy cogeneration equipment reduces carbon dioxide emissions by over 90 percent, making the Reichstag the first ecologically responsible parliament building anywhere in the world.

Principal consultants: Ove Arup & Partners, structural engineers for competition scheme; Schlaich Bergermann & Partner and Leonhardt Andrä und Partner, structural engineers for final scheme; Kaiser Bautechnik, Kuehn Associates, Amstein und Walthert, Fischer Energie und Haustechnik, Planungsgruppe Karnasch-Hackstein, mechanical, electrical, and environmental engineers; Acanthus, conservation consultants; Davis Langdon & Everest, cost consultants

Foster and Partners Principal Projects

1964	Forest Road Extension, East Horsley, Surrey
1964	Mews Houses, Murray Mews, Camden Town, London
1964	Waterfront Housing, Cornwall
1964–66	Skybreak House, Radlett, Hertfordshire
1964	Cockpit, Pil Creek, Cornwall
1964–66	Creek Vean House, Feock, Cornwall
1965–66	Reliance Controls Limited, Swindon, Wiltshire
1965	Housing for Wates, Coulsden, Surrey
1965	Henrion Studio, London
1967	Newport School Competition
1968–69	Fred Olsen Limited Amenity Centre, Millwall
1969	Factory Systems Studies
1969	Masterplan for Fred Olsen Limited, Millwall
1970–71	Fred Olsen Limited Passenger Terminal, Millwall
1970–71	Computer Technology Limited, Hemel Hempstead, Hertfordshire
1970–71	IBM Advance Head Office, Cosham, Hampshire
1970	Air-Supported Structure for Computer Technology Limited, Hertfordshire
1971–75	Willis Faber and Dumas Head Office, Ipswich, Suffolk
1971–73	Special Care Unit, Hackney, London
1971	Foster Associates Studio, London
1971	Samuel Beckett Theatre, St. Peter's College, Oxford
1971	Climatroffice
1971–72	Retail & Leisure Studies, Liverpool, Exeter & Badhoevedorp
1972–73	Orange Hand Shops for Burton Group
1972–73	Modern Art Glass Limited, Thamesmead, Kent
1973–75	Low Rise Housing, Bean Hill, Milton Keynes, Buckinghamshire
1973–74	Headquarters for VW Audi NSU & Mercedes Benz, Milton Keynes, Buckinghamshire
1973–77	Aluminium Extrusion Plant for SAPA, Tibshelf, Derby
1974–78	Sainsbury Centre for Visual Arts, UEA, Norwich, Norfolk
1974–75	Palmerston Special School, Liverpool
1974	Country Club and Marina, Son, Norway
1974	Travel Agency for Fred Olsen Limited, London
1974	Offices for Fred Olsen Limited, Vestby, Norway
1975–76	Regional Planning Studies for Island of Gomera, Canaries
1975	Fred Olsen Gate Redevelopment, Oslo, Norway
1976–77	Masterplan for St. Helier Harbour, Jersey
1977–79	Technical Park for IBM, Greenford, Middlesex
1977–79	Transportation Interchange for LTE, Hammersmith, London
1978	London Gliding Club, Dunstable Downs
1978–79	Foster Residence, Hampstead, London
1978	Proposals for International Energy Expo, Knoxville, Tennessee
1978	Open House Community Project, Cwmbran, Wales
1978	Whitney Museum Development Project, New York
1979–86	New Headquarters for the Hongkong and Shanghai Banking Corporation, Hong Kong *
1979	Granada Entertainment Centre, Milton Keynes
1979	Shop for Joseph, Knightsbridge, London
1980–83	Parts Distribution Centre for Renault UK limited, Swindon, Wiltshire
1980	Planning Studies for Statue Square, Hong Kong
1980	Students Union Building, University College, London
1981	Foster Associates office, Great Portland Street, London
1981	Internal Systems, Furniture for Foster Associates
1981–86	National Indoor Athletics Stadium, Frankfurt, Germany *
1981–91	Third London Airport Stansted, Essex:
	– New Terminal Building
	– New Airside Satellites
	– Landside Airside Coach Stations
	– Terminal Zone Masterplan
1981	Competition for Billingsgate Fish Market, London
1982–85	New Radio Centre for BBC, London *
1982	Autonomous Dwelling (with Dr. Richard Buckminster Fuller)
1982	Competition for Headquarters of Humana Inc., Louisville, Kentucky
1984–93	Centre d'Art Contemporain et Médiathèque, Carré d'Art, Nîmes,* France
1984–86	IBM Head office, Major Refit, Cosham, Hants
1985–91	Sackler Galleries, Royal Academy of Arts, London
1985–87	Furniture system for Tecno, Italy
1985	New offices for IBM at Greenford, Middlesex
1986–90	Riverside Development, Apartments and Offices for Foster and Partners
1986	Salle de Spectacles, Nancy, France

1986	Headquarters for Televisa, Mexico City, Mexico	1989-91	Street furniture for Decaux, Paris
1986	Shop for Katharine Hamnett, Brompton Road, London	1989	Terminal 5 Heathrow Airport, London
1986	New York Marina	1989-91	British Rail station, Stansted Airport, Stansted, Essex
1987	Hotel and Club, Knightsbridge, London	1989	Technology Centres, Edinburgh and Glasgow, Scotland
1987-97	American Air Museum, Duxford, Essex	1989-97	Kite! chair for Tecno, Italy
1987	Redevelopment masterplan, Kings Cross, London*	1989	Office building for Jacob's Island Co., Docklands, London
1987-89	Riverside housing and light industrial complex, Hammersmith, London	1990-93	Private House, Corsica, France
		1990-93	Motoryacht for Japanese client
1987-91	Century Tower office building, Bunkyo-ku, Tokyo, Japan	1990	Office building DS2 at Canary Wharf, Docklands, London*
1987-92	Private House, Japan	1990	Masterplan for Berlin
1987-89	Offices for Stanhope Securities, Stockley Park, Uxbridge, Middlesex	1990	Masterplan for Cannes, France
		1990	Masterplan for Nîmes, France
1987	Turin Airport, Turin, Italy	1990-95	Law Faculty of Cambridge University, Cambridge*
1987	Hotel for La Fondiaria, Florence, Italy	1990	Office building for Fonta, Toulouse, France
1987	Shopping Centre for Savacentre near Southampton	1990	Refurbishment of Brittanic House, City of London
1987	Bunka Radio Station, Yarai Cho, Tokyo, Japan	1990	Hotel du Département, Marseilles, France
1987	Competition for Paternoster Square redevelopment, London	1990	Congress hall, San Sebastian, Spain
1988-90	ITN Headquarters, London	1990	Trade Fair Centre, Berlin
1988-97	Microelectronic Centre, Duisburg, Germany	1990	Stage set for Paul McCartney
1988-93	Business Promotion Centre, Duisburg, Germany	1991	Private Houses, Japan
1988-93	Telematic Centre, Duisburg, Germany	1991-92	Cladding system for Jansen Vegla Glass, Switzerland/Germany
1988	Sackler Galleries, Jerusalem, Israel	1991	Masterplan for Greenwich, London
1988-91	Crescent Wing at the Sainsbury Centre for Visual Arts, UEA, Norwich, Norfolk	1991-99	Masterplan for Duisburg Harbour, Germany*
		1991	Paint Factory, Frankfurt Colloquium, Frankfurt
1988-92	Telecommunications Tower, Torre de Collserola, Barcelona*	1991-97	New Headquarters for Commerzbank, Frankfurt*
1988-95	Bilbao Metro, Bilbao, Spain *	1991	Gateway office building to Spitalfields Redevelopment, London
1988	City of London Heliport, London		
1988	Shop for Esprit, Sloane Street, London	1991-93	Lycée Polyvalent Régional Albert Camus, Fréjus, France*
1988	Contract carpet and tile design for Vorwerk, Germany	1991	Napp Laboratories, Cambridge
1988	Kansai Airport, Japan	1991	University of Cambridge Institute of Criminology, Cambridge
1988	Pont D'Austerlitz, bridge across the river Seine, Paris		
1988	Offices for Stanhope Securities, London Wall City of London	1991	Office building for Stanhope Properties and County Natwest, London
1988	Holiday Inn, The Hague, Holland		
1989	Passenger Concourse building for British Rail, King's Cross	1991	New headquarters and retail building for Sanei Corp., Makuhari, Japan
1989	Millennium Tower, Japan		
1989-91	Offices for Stanhope Properties, Chiswick Park Development	1991-96	New headquarters for Agiplan, Mulheim, Germany
1989-92	New library for Cranfield University,* Bedfordshire	1991-93	New headquarters for Obunsha Corp., Yarai Cho, Tokyo, Japan
1989	Planning studies for the City of Cambridge		
1989	Congress Hall, Toulouse, France	1991-98	Canary Wharf Station for the Jubilee Line underground extension*
1989	Apartments and offices, New York		

1991–	Viaduct for Rennes, France*
1992–94	Solar Electric Vehicle, Kew, London
1992	New York Police Academy, New York
1992–96	Offices for Electricité de France, Bordeaux, France
1992	Headquarters Factory and Warehouse for Tecno, Valencia, Spain
1992–99	New German Parliament, Reichstag, Berlin*
1992	Tower Place Offices, City of London
1992–98	Kowloon Canton Railway Station/Terminal Hong Kong
1992–98	HACTL Air Cargo building, Chek Lap Kok, Hong Kong
1992	Yokohama Masterplan, Japan
1992	Business Park, Berlin*
1992	Manchester Olympic Bid Masterplan*
1992–93	Refurbishment and addition to the Hamlyn House, Chelsea, London
1992	Spandau Bridge, Berlin
1992–96	Thames Valley Business Park, Reading, England*
1992	Station Poterie, Rennes, France
1992–94	Addition to Joslyn Art Museum, Omaha, Nebraska*
1992–94	School of Physiotherapy, Southampton, England
1992–94	Private house in Germany
1992	High bay warehouse Lüdenscheid, Germany
1992	Masterplan for Lüdenscheid, Germany
1992	Houston Museum of Fine Arts, Houston, Texas
1992–97	Ground Transportation Centre, Chek Lap Kok, Hong Kong
1992–97	New airport at Chek Lap Kok, Hong Kong*
1992–93	Marine Simulator, Rotterdam, The Netherlands
1992	Masterplan for Wilhelminapier, Rotterdam, The Netherlands
1992	Masterplan for Imperial College, London
1992	World Trade Centre, Berlin
1992–97	Design Centre Essen, Germany
1992–92	Clore Theatre, Imperial College, London
1992	Shops and franchises for Cacharel, France
1992–99	Musée de Préhistoire, Gorges du Verdon, Quinson, France*
1993	New office and railway development Kuala Lumpur
1993–95	Forth Valley Community Care Village, Scotland
1993	Holborn Circus offices, London
1993	Viaduct, Millau, France*
1993–	
2000	Al Faisaliah Complex, Riyadh, Saudi Arabia*

1993–	Headquarters for ARAG 2000, Düsseldorf, Germany
1993	Masterplan for Lisbon Expo 98, Portugal*
1993	Masterplan for Corfu, Greece
1993	Hong Kong Convention and Exhibition Centre, Hong Kong
1993	London School of Economics Library, London
1993	Tennis Centre, Manchester
1993–98	Congress Centre, Valencia, Spain
1993	Headquarters for Timex, Connecticut
1993	Street Lighting for Decaux
1993–97	MTR Platform Edge Screens, Signage and Furniture, Hong Kong
1993–95	Wind Turbine energy generator, Germany
1993	South Kensington Millennium Project—Albertopolis*
1993	National Gallery of Scottish Art, Glasgow
1993	Oresund Bridge, Copenhagen
1993	Imperial War Museum, Hartlepool*
1993	Exhibition Halls, Villepinte, Paris
1993	Urban Design at Porte Maillot, Paris
1993	Medieval Centre for Chartres, France
1993	Masterplanning Studies for Gare d'Austerlitz Station, Paris
1993	New Headquarters for Credit du Nord, Paris
1994	Telecommunications Facility, Santiago de Compostela, Spain
1994	Criterion Place Development, Leeds*
1994	Visions for Europe, Düsseldorf, Germany
1994–98	Faculty of Management, Robert Gordon University, Aberdeen, Scotland
1994–98	Imperial College Bio-Medical Sciences Building, London
1994–	
2000	Great Court, British Museum Redevelopment, London*
1994	Cardiff Bay Opera House, Cardiff, Wales
1994	Grande Stade, St. Denis, Paris
1994	Centre de la Mémoire, Oradour sur Glanes, France
1994	Casino-Kursaal, Oostende, Belgium
1994	Bangkok Airport, Thailand
1994	Zhongshan Guangzhou, Retail and Office development, China*
1994–96	SeaLife Centre, Birmingham
1994–95	SeaLife Centre, Blankenberge, Belgium
1995	Moorfields Offices, City of London

1995–98	Transport Interchange, Greenwich
1995–99	Medical Research Laboratory, Stanford University, California*
1995	Office and Showroom for Samsung Motors, Korea*
1995– 2000	Housing and offices Gerling Ring, Cologne
1995–98	Multimedia Centre, Hamburg, Germany*
1995	Door furniture for Fusital, Italy
1995–98	Swimming pool and Fitness Centre, Stanmore, Middlesex
1995	World Port Centre, Rotterdam, The Netherlands
1995	Competition for I G Metall Headquarters, Frankfurt, Germany
1995– 2000	National Botanic Gardens for Wales, Middleton Hall, Wales
1995	Bank Headquarters, Dubai
1995	Private House in Connecticut
1995	Cladding System for Technal, France
1995	Solar City Linz, Austria
1995	Master Plan for Regensburg, Germany
1995– 2001	Headquarters for Daewoo Electronics, Seoul, Korea
1995–97	New Conference and Exhibition Facilities for SECC, Glasgow
1995	Club House, Silverstone Race Track, Silverstone
1995	Oita Stadium, Japan
1995–99	Jiu Shi Tower, Shanghai, China
1995	Murr Tower, Offices, Beirut*
1995	Offices for LIFFE, London
1996	Wood Street offices, City of London
1996	World Squares for All Master Plan for Central London*
1996–99	Millennium Bridge, London*
1996–98	Service Stations for Repsol, Spain
1996	Gresham Street offices, City of London*
1996–99	Office development for Citibank, London
1996	Stadium design and Masterplan for Wembley Stadium, London*
1996	Arsta Bridge, Stockholm, Sweden*
1996	Oxford University Library, Oxford
1996	Redevelopment of Treasury Offices, London
1996–98	Offices for Slough Estates, Ascot, Berkshire
1996–97	Offices for Slough Estates, Bath Road, Slough, Middlesex
1996	International Rail Terminal, St. Pancras, London
1996	London Millennium Tower offices, City of London*
1997	Mixed Use Development, Battersea, London
1997	Masterplan for Durban, South Africa
1997	Parkview offices, Singapore
1997	Somapah Station, Singapore
1997	Feasibility studies for Luton Airport
1997	Masterplan for Madrid
1997	Bankers Trust Tower, Sydney, Australia
1997	Headquarters for Decaux, Brentford
1997	Headquarters for Electronic Arts, UK*
1997	Regional Music Centre, Gateshead*
1997	Moor House offices, City of London
1997	Housing development for Rialto, Wandsworth, London
1997	Feasibility Study for the Roundhouse, Camden, London
1997	Reading Business Park for the Prudential, Berkshire
1997	Department Store for Selfridges, Glasgow
1998	Warsaw Hines
1998	TAG McLaren Research and Development Centre, Woking
1998	GLA Building, London
1998	London Bridge Masterplan

* denotes winner of national or international competition

Photography Credits

All drawings appear courtesy of Foster and Partners. The photographs appear courtesy of the photographers or institutions, as noted below.

Andrew Ward: page 6

Rudi Meisel: pages 12, 15, 18, 228, 232–34

Norman Foster: pages 20, 20–21, 22–23, 25, 26, 88

Gus Coral: page 28–29

Tim Street-Porter: pages 30, 31, 32, 33, 34, 36–37, 42, 45, 52–53, 57

Courtesy of Fred Olsen: page 38

Richard Einzig: page 40–41

Ken Kirkwood: pages 44–45, 46, 49, 50–51, 58–59, 60, 61, 62,
120–21, 124,

Richard Davies: pages 70–71, 72, 89, 90, 103–4, 107, 108, 114, 116,
117, 119, 122–23, 126, 155, 162, 169, 193, 197, 200–201, 200,
202, 221, 222–23, 224, 228–29

John Donat: pages 54, 56

Ben Johnson: pages 65, 161

Dennis Gilbert: pages 66, 67, 98, 99, 101, 112, 125, 128, 131,
132–33, 134, 136–37, 138–39, 139, 141, 142, 144, 149, 178–79,
180, 181, 182, 195, 204, 206–7, 210–11, 212, 214, 231

Alastair Hunter: page 69

Ian Lambot: pages 74, 78–81, 170, 172, 175, 177

Martin Charles: page 82

Mishima: page 83

Tecno: pages 84, 85, 87

Martin Pawley: page 91

James H. Morris: pages 92–93, 95

Foster and Partners: page 97

Michel Porro: page 140–41

Nigel Young: pages 111, 146, 147, 150–51, 152–54, 171, 184, 185,
186–87, 188, 205, 208–9, 209, 218

John Edward Linden: pages 157, 192, 194

Xavier Basiana Vers: page 158–59

Obayashi: pages 164, 166

Tom Miller: page 168

Jens Willebrand: page 174

Paul Raftery: page 212–13

Nigel Curry: page 216–17

The British Museum: pages 225, 226